ACCESS YOUR ONLINE RESOURCES

Becoming an Autism-Affirming Primary School is accompanied by a number of printable online materials, designed to ensure this resource best supports your professional needs

Go to https://resourcecentre.routledge.com/speechmark and click on the cover of this book

Answer the question prompt using your copy of the book to gain access to the online content.

BECOMING AN AUTISM-AFFIRMING PRIMARY SCHOOL

This accessible guide explores what an autism-affirming primary school should be like, from the perspective of autistic pupils, introducing a tool to gather pupil voice and sharing a toolbox of strategies informed and requested by autistic children themselves. The book presents a fun and engaging approach, the three houses, which can be used with autistic children to generate a greater understanding of how they are experiencing school and how they may be masking their difficulties.

Chapters focus on common themes, from developing a shared, positive understanding of autism throughout the school, to consideration of the classroom environment, hidden support, homework and routines. By identifying simple adjustments to practice, schools can create a more positive experience for autistic children, building self-advocacy and helping to alleviate feelings of anxiety. The book includes a wealth of easy-to-implement, practical strategies that place an emphasis on whole-school approaches, as well as opportunities for readers to reflect on their current practice. Quotes from autistic children, describing their experiences, are woven throughout the book.

Becoming an Autism-Affirming Primary School keeps the voices of autistic pupils at its core and is a valuable read for primary school teachers, SENCos and senior leaders to ensure they are offering much-needed support for autistic children, which will also be of benefit to their non-autistic peers. Parents may find it useful to generate an understanding of how their autistic children might be experiencing school and autistic children themselves may find the narrative from other autistic children valuable.

Melanie Cunningham has enjoyed working with autistic children for many years. She is currently an Assistant Headteacher and has previously led a Specialist Resource Provision for autistic children. Her research findings on what an autism-affirming primary school should be like, from the perspective of autistic pupils, were published in the International Journal of Inclusive Education. She has spoken at national and international conferences and has a Masters in Special and Inclusive Education from University College, London.

BECOMING AN AUTISM-AFFIRMING PRIMARY SCHOOL

How to Listen to Our Autistic Pupils to Create Meaningful Change

Melanie Cunningham

Routledge
Taylor & Francis Group

LONDON AND NEW YORK

Designed cover image: @getty

First published 2025
by Routledge
4 Park Square, Milton Park, Abingdon, Oxon OX14 4RN

and by Routledge
605 Third Avenue, New York, NY 10158

Routledge is an imprint of the Taylor & Francis Group, an informa business

© 2025 Melanie Cunningham

British Library Cataloguing-in-Publication Data
A catalogue record for this book is available from the British Library

ISBN: 978-1-032-50011-9 (hbk)
ISBN: 978-1-032-50008-9 (pbk)
ISBN: 978-1-003-39649-9 (ebk)

DOI: 10.4324/9781003396499

Typeset in Interstate
by SPi Technologies India Pvt Ltd (Straive)

Access the Support Material: https://resourcecentre.routledge.com/speechmark

For David, William, Anna, Lucy ... truly

CONTENTS

FIGURES

TABLES

Chapter 4

Chapter 5

Chapter 6

ACKNOWLEDGEMENTS

Enormous thanks to the many children and young people who have so willingly contributed to this book. Your insights are astonishing and serve as a powerful testimony to the importance of listening to and acting upon pupil voice. You are all formidable advocates, and I am certain that your testimonies will empower others, who read this book, to change how we listen to and respond to the thoughts, views and feelings of pupils. I hope that change will come. You have taught me many things and the most valuable of these is that autism is a very special thing.

While all contributions are of equal value, the first contributors, 'Will', Eleanor, Jack and Toby were the inspiration for this book. I must acknowledge, Will, whose declaration, all those years ago, led to me researching and writing this book.

Thank you also to the families, parents and carers of the contributors who consented, enabled and facilitated my many interviews.

I have been supported throughout the process by my illustrious colleagues. I am particularly grateful to Ciaran Beatty and Marie-Claire McGregor Ridley who have been with me every step of the way as we continue to strive for schools which are truly autism-affirming. Thank you also to Catherine Byrne, whose support is always invaluable. Individual members of staff are too numerous to mention but I am acutely aware that the members of staff who support our children on an individual basis are often their greatest advocates.

My editors at Routledge Education, Taylor & Francis, Clare Ashworth and Molly Kavanagh, have guided me through the writing and editing process and I am immensely grateful to them. It was Clare who had the insight to recognise that we are missing books which are centred around pupil voice.

Thank you to my reviewers who anonymously scrutinised the initial proposal for the book and subsequently read the final manuscript. Your input has resulted in a better book. Daisy Loyd not only gave up her valuable time to review my manuscript, but she also supervised my Master's thesis, encouraged me to submit it for publication and shaped my thinking on how we can, and should, engage with our pupils.

My mother and late father have passed on a lifelong love of learning, a ferocious work ethic and have always encouraged me. Thank you.

Finally to my family, my 'backroom staff'. My husband David who has helped me to keep all my plates spinning. He has picked them up and glued them back together when I have dropped them, handed them back to me or kept hold of them. I know you won't believe me when I say 'Anyone who sees me go anywhere near a boat again, ever ...' To my amazing children William, Anna and Lucy who have not minded when I have smashed plates and have never passed comment when I have spent more time with other people's children than I have with them. I am astonishingly proud of you all. Thank you ... truly.

Chapter one

Introduction and aims of the book

How the book came about

'This school is 100% NOT autistic-friendly', declared a Year Four autistic pupil. We printed his quote and displayed it in our staff room, recognising that we needed to take some form of affirmative action. The pupil's declaration was a catalyst for change in our school, as we reflected on what we could do to gather our autistic pupils' views, thoughts and feelings to understand how they were experiencing school (Cunningham, 2020). We thought we were doing a decent job of supporting our autistic pupils, but that was, of course, our perspective.

This book combines research, practice, advocacy and pupil voice to understand how autistic pupils experience school. I explain the importance of using pupil voice to understand the adaptations and adjustments which we need to make in schools and elsewhere. I consider the right for every child to be heard and highlight the poor outcomes for autistic children and young people across multiple sectors, including school. The methodology used to gather the views, thoughts and feelings of autistic pupils in a meaningful way is discussed, as well as how to adapt practice in response to pupil voice. Following a research project at our school, a number of changes have been made as part of a whole-school approach. These adaptations and adjustments have had a positive impact on our autistic and non-autistic pupils alike. The emphasis throughout is on pupil voice and all the adaptations and adjustments have been requested by the pupils themselves.

The purpose of the book is two-fold

- Introduce a tool which we can use to gather autistic pupil voice so that we can understand how our pupils are experiencing school.
- By listening to our pupils, we should be able to generate an understanding of the adaptations and adjustments which we need to make to enable a positive school experience, improve the outcomes of our autistic pupils and develop autism-affirming schools. I highlight the adaptations and adjustments which autistic pupils are themselves requesting. The consistency of the narratives of a large number of autistic pupils, who have shared their views, thoughts and feelings on school, should give us the confidence to understand the changes which we should make, within our schools.

DOI: 10.4324/9781003396499-1

Chapter outline

In this chapter, I consider how autism is described, experienced, identified and diagnosed, the impact of self-advocacy on language and the evolving perspectives as we shift away from a medical-deficit model to a strength-based, identity-first approach. The chapter closes with a number of biographies from some of the children and young people who have, so willingly, contributed to this book.

In Chapter 2, I consider why it is important to understand and act on the perspectives of autistic pupils. I consider the historic failing to uncover the voices of autistic children and young people and how this has impacted on their lives and their right to be heard, as citizens. I consider the personal perspectives and autographical reflections of autistic adults on their school experiences and the impact on their lives of not being listened to. As the number of autism diagnoses continues to rise, an increasing number of children and young people are being unintentionally let down by schools, further and higher education institutions, employers and health providers. I reflect on how this is all too often due to a lack of understanding of autism.

The three houses approach, the methodology used to gather the views, thoughts and feelings of the children and young people, is explained in Chapter 3.

Chapters 4 and 5 move on to reflect on how we can use our pupils' perspectives to support teachers, friends and peers in generating a greater understanding of autism and of our autistic pupils. I reflect on implications for practice, alongside a toolbox of strategies, and introduce a programme which can support our pupils in generating a greater understanding of themselves as autistic children and young people, through a strength-based approach. I also consider how to use the pupils' perspectives to support us in generating a greater understanding of autism in general and of our autistic pupils specifically to develop a whole-school, inclusive approach where diversity is the norm. The chapters conclude with quotes from autistic children and young people. These narratives serve as a powerful testimony and emphasise why we need to take affirmative action.

Further reflections on what an autism-affirming school be like from the pupils' perspectives are considered in Chapter 6. Consideration is given to implications for practice alongside a toolbox of strategies, which are simple, cheap and easy to implement. All the strategies were requested by the children themselves and aid our understanding of the support which is needed and how to deliver it in a way that is acceptable to the pupils. The emphasis is on a whole-school approach. The chapter also concludes with the voices of autistic children and young people.

In the final chapter, I draw some conclusions on how we may begin to create autism-affirming schools, from our pupils' perspectives. I stress that all the adaptations and adjustments discussed in this book are requested by the pupils themselves and may, therefore, give us a unique perspective into what autism-affirming school should be like. I share personal reflections and leave the last word to four of our pupils whose views, thoughts and feelings on their experience of school were the catalyst for this book.

What is autism?

I am often asked by teachers, children and parents: 'What is autism?' There is no easy response to this question. Autism is a complex developmental condition. Put as simply as possible, autism affects the way an individual communicates with, and experiences, the world around them. It is a way of perceiving, processing and interacting with the world and is described as a spectrum condition. This means that while autistic individuals share certain characteristics, they are highly individual in their strengths, interests, needs and preferences. As a result, autistic individuals often express themselves by communicating and socially interacting in ways that are similar to other autistic people. Autism is many things but, put simply, it is one way of viewing and experiencing the world.

We are starting to understand that a lack of understanding of autism is having a significant impact on autistic people. Prizant (2022) highlights that the actions of non-autistic people can be helpful and unhelpful to autistic people. As I will highlight throughout this book, it is often a lack of understanding from non-autistic people which is affecting the lives of autistic children and young people. 'Autism isn't an illness. It's a different way of being human ... To help [autistic children and young people], we don't need to change them or fix them. We need to work to understand them, **and then change what we do**.' In other words, autism is a different way of thinking and being 'uniquely human' (Prizant, 2022, bold added).

What is neurodiversity?

The term neurodiversity is increasingly being used in schools and other settings and is preferable to many. It could be considered as an umbrella term; autism is under the canopy. The term is increasingly being pioneered by self-advocacy groups as an inclusive, nonjudgemental term to promote equality, equity and the inclusion of neurological minorities. The term is advantageous to many as it was created within the community it describes, rather than being imposed upon it from outside the group (Wise, 2024).

Like autism, neurodiversity is increasingly understood as a form of human diversity. Baumer and Frueh (2021) describe neurodiversity as 'the idea that people experience and interact with the world around them in many different ways; there is no one "right" way of thinking, learning, and behaving, and differences are not viewed as deficits'.

Jon Adams, a contemporary artist and researcher who often references his autism says: 'Autism is an innate way of thinking ... neurodiversity is just another form of being human' (Wood, 2019, p. 36).

Kabie Brook, cofounder and current chair of Autism Rights Group Highland, states that 'Autism is part of natural neurodiversity, a neurodivergence amongst many (I am unconvinced of a true neurotypical majority)' (Wood, 2019, p. 36).

Neurodiversity recognises that neurological differences do not need to be disadvantageous but the difficulties which autistic children and young people experience are often the result of a lack of understanding and empathy of their experiences as autistic individuals. It is becoming increasingly obvious that we need to start to generate a greater understanding of autism to enable us to support our autistic pupils in school.

A brief history of autism, prevalence rates and increasing numbers

We are only just beginning to develop an understanding of autism and, therefore, of prevalence rates. A brief look at the history of autism finds that autism was first identified in 1943 when Kanner described specific patterns of behaviour, which he referred to as early infantile autism (Kanner, 1943). He considered this to be a rare condition. In 1979, Wing and Gould found a larger group of children, approximately 20 in every 10,000, whom they described as being on the 'autism spectrum' (Wing and Gould, 1979). Having worked with autistic children and young people for over 30 years, Wolff started to highlight how a lack of understanding impacted on these children, highlighting that they often have a difficult time at school, and they need recognition and understanding from their parents and teachers (Wolff, 1995). Wolff found the prevalence rate to be around 71 autistic children ten thousand.

As more is understood about the autism spectrum, prevalence rates continue to rise.

We do not know how many people are autistic. Reported prevalence rates have risen each decade since Kanner first identified autism. Although prevalence rates of between 0.6 per cent and 1.5 per cent remained fairly consistent through the twentieth century and the start of the twenty-first century, as most of us are aware, prevalence rates are now on the rise. This means that an increasing number of pupils are at risk of being misunderstood and let down by multiple sectors, including school. This misunderstanding of autism is evident in reported prevalence rates, which continue to vary greatly.

Russell et al. compared the rates of autism recorded in GP records in England. Her research looked at the records of over nine million patients from GP practices in 2021. She reported that the number of people diagnosed as autistic has jumped by 787% in the past two decades, between 1998 and 2018.

In 2021, the BBC ran a headline: Autism: Almost one in 20 [5 per cent] NI [Northern Ireland] schoolchildren have diagnosis [of autism]. The report recognised that an increased awareness as a result of the Autism Act NI, which was passed in 2011, as a potential reason for this rise in diagnoses.

In the USA, the Centers for Disease Control and Prevention (CDC) issued a press release reporting that one in 36 (2.8 per cent) 8-year-old children have been identified with autism spectrum disorder (ASD), according to an analysis published today in CDC's Morbidity and Mortality Weekly Report (MMWR). The new findings are higher than the previous 2018 estimate that found a prevalence of 1 in 44 (2.3 per cent) (CDC.gov, 2023).

The British Medical Association (Mehlmann-Wicks, 2020) reports a lower prevalence rate and estimates that around 700,000 people and one in 100 children in the UK have a diagnosis of autism. Similarly, the National Autistic Society (2023) reports that more than one in 100 people are on the autism spectrum and there are around 700,000 autistic adults and children in the UK. Such a prevalence rate would mean that, in a one-form entry school, around two of the pupils would be autistic. I wonder whether this aligns with our experiences of school.

Autistica.org.uk report a higher prevalence rate and believe that around one in 67 people in the UK is autistic and recognises that many adults (particularly females) have never been diagnosed. The Autism Education Trust suggest that one in 41 children is autistic. At the National Autistic Society conference in 2023, Dr Wenn Lawson suggested that the prevalence rate could be as high as one in 38. We may be moving in the right direction!

These varying prevalence rates may mean that the number of autistic children and young people in the UK is inaccurate and unrepresented. We still have a lot to learn about autism and as we understand more, we recognise that autism is far more prevalent than previously recorded prevalence rates may suggest. I am often asked whether there are more autistic individuals per se. We simply do not know the answer to this question.

The increase in prevalence rates is likely to be due to a combination of an increased understanding and recognition of autism, increased reporting, and broader application of the autism diagnosis, particularly for females. Any increase in numbers could be attributed to a reduction in the stigma that has historically been associated with autism which has resulted in increasing numbers seeking a diagnosis. As a number of well-known autistic individuals have proudly shared their autism diagnosis in recent years, autism has moved into mainstream media and social media channels. An effective self-advocacy movement may also be having an impact. However, an actual increase in autism incidence cannot be ruled out.

Increased prevalence rates may also reflect the fact that parents may be seeking a diagnosis in order to access the additional resources which may enable improved outcomes in school for their child or young person. Many parents and carers have to battle for their child to be diagnosed in the hope that a formal diagnosis may make it easier to access scant resources they believe are needed to improve their child's experience of school. Many parents of autistic children start their journey in school using the language of 'battle' and 'fight' and are exhausted by their experience of the system by the time their child starts compulsory education. The 2022 Government Green Paper recognised that parents' confidence in the system is in decline and too many parents have lost faith in a system that is not sufficiently responsive to them, which is increasingly adversarial, and in which they face long waiting times to access information and support for their children and young people, in schools and beyond.

'Getting their child that superb education that everyone deserves can feel like a full-time job' (Minister for Children, Families and Wellbeing, Claire Coutinho 2023 press release).

As prevalence rates continue to rise, it becomes increasingly important that we find ways to uncover the voice of autistic children and young people and understand how to meet their needs. Failure to do this will result in an increasing number of autistic children and young people being let down across multiple sectors, including schools.

Diagnostic criteria and language of the DSM-5

How is autism diagnosed in the UK? The American Psychiatric Association Diagnostic and Statistical Manual of Mental Disorders (DSM-5) remains the standard that healthcare and medical providers use to diagnose autism in the UK and nationally (American Psychiatric Association, 2013). The DSM-5 states that autistic individuals will typically experience challenges with social interaction and communication and restricted/repetitive behaviours and may also experience the sensory aspects of the world in an unusual or extreme way. The DSM-5 does not mention anything about increased levels of stress and anxiety. Neither does it mention strengths and positive attributes associated with being autistic. This may go some way to explaining why autism has been, and continues to be, so misunderstood and viewed negatively by so many.

The DSM-5 is a medical, deficit model used to diagnose autism. It uses negative vocabulary and measures characteristics against the 'normal'. As a way of generating an understanding of how autism has been viewed, I have included the DSM-5 diagnostic criteria below, and high-lighted the overtly negative vocabulary used throughout (American Psychiatric Association 2013).

> **Persistent deficits** in social communication and social interaction.
>
> **Deficits** in social-emotional reciprocity, such as **abnormal** social approach and **failure of normal** back-and-forth conversation, **reduced** sharing of interests, emotions, **failure** to initiate or respond to social interactions.
>
> **Deficits** in nonverbal communicative behaviours used for social interaction, including **abnormalities** in eye contact and body language or **deficits** in understanding and use of gestures, to a **total lack of** facial expressions and nonverbal communication.
>
> **Deficits** in developing, maintaining, and understanding relationships, ranging from difficulties adjusting behaviour to suit various social contexts, to difficulties in sharing imaginative play or in making friends, to **absence of** interest in peers.
>
> **Restricted**, repetitive patterns of behaviour, interests or activities.
>
> **Stereotyped** or repetitive motor movements, use of objects, or speech.

Insistence on sameness, inflexible adherence to routines, or ritualised patterns of behaviour.

> Highly restricted, fixated interests that are **abnormal** in intensity or focus.
>
> Hyper- or hypo-response to sensory input or unusual interests in sensory aspects of the environment.

The criteria of the DSM-5 describe autism purely in terms of deficits, causing many people to misunderstand autism. Dr Engelbrecht (2021), who was herself diagnosed as autistic in her forties, raises concerns about the language used in the DSM-5. She notes that, when describing the diagnostic criteria for autism, the DSM-5 uses language that is confusing, ableist and pathology-based. Engelbrecht explains that the DSM is a diagnostic manual of pathologies, thereby focusing on the negative aspects of the condition, while ignoring the positive traits.

Most parents of children and young people who are diagnosed as autistic will not read the DSM-5 criteria, either before or after the diagnosis, and will, therefore, be unaware of the language used. Although we are making small steps to viewing autism more positively, as medical and healthcare practitioners are increasingly referring to autism as a condition (Autistic Spectrum Condition) rather than a disorder (Autistic Spectrum Disorder), we are still some way from re-framing autism to better reflect the experiences of autistic people, having listened to their voices.

Asperger's syndrome as a diagnostic term

In 2013, the American Psychiatric Association removed Asperger's disorder from the new DSM-5. While the concept of autism as a spectrum condition is important, it is now agreed that what was referred to as Asperger's disorder is part of the autism spectrum and there is no need for a separate term. The DSM-5 now has only one broad category for autism: ASD, which replaces all the previous diagnoses, including Asperger's.

One reason that the term Asperger's was removed from DSM5 was to avoid the misconception that Asperger's is a different condition to autism. The change reflects new research which indicates that there was little consistency in the way Asperger's was applied when considering a diagnosis and arbitrary boundaries are unhelpful.

Second, Asperger's often implied a certain level of intelligence that might not be assumed in a person who is diagnosed as autistic, though this assumption is incorrect. Furthermore, the challenges that people living with Asperger's may encounter were not always recognised, resulting in them being denied much needed help and support.

Finally, the term Asperger's is now considered controversial due to the uncovering of the history of the Austrian psychiatrist Hans Asperger, who the disorder is named after (Czech, 2018). People who have identified with a diagnosis of Asperger's throughout their life may now find the revelations about Hans Asperger upsetting and choose to identify as autistic, despite their previous diagnosis. Of course, self-identity is unique to each individual.

The importance of a strength-based approach

In part, due to the autistic self-advocacy movement, the autistic narrative is slowly beginning to change. Huntley et al. (2019) carried out research for Autistica, a UK-based autism research charity established to support the needs of autistic individuals and the autistic community. They acknowledge the emerging science for a strengths-based approach to supporting autistic children and young people and recognise that they are so much more than the challenges that are, all too often, used to define them. Huntley et al. also suggest that we need to develop a greater understanding of how to support each child or young person with their unique profile of strengths and difficulties, recognising that we are all unique.

The following is a series of quotes from autistic advocates, explaining their frustration at how autism is often misunderstood by non-autistic individuals and the difficulties that this lack of understanding creates for them. I wonder whether pupils in school today would have a similar narrative. Their powerful testimonies highlight the need to generate a greater understanding of what we need to do to support our autistic pupils in school.

> It is a serious problem that many individuals on the spectrum grow up regularly hearing about what their problems are. It can have a detrimental effect on how they see themselves. Using a strengths-based approach from the outset, so they also understand that they have amazing strengths, would help to give them a much more balanced outlook.
>
> *
>
> Autism is not a disability. Apart from the ones that society has put in the way – there are no disadvantages.
>
> (George in Wood, 2019, p. 38)

> I identify as a disabled person because in a society which is mainly non-autistic my needs often aren't accommodated. I am disabled by a neuronormative world.
>
> (Kabie in Wood, 2019, p. 38)

> People's non-understanding of autism is a disability.
>
> (Jon in Wood, 2019, p. 39)

We have historically focused too much on 'impairment' and deficit, often leading to detrimental outcomes for autistic children and young people across multiple sectors, including schools. Huntley et al. (2019) advocate changing the narrative and suggest embracing a strengths-based approach to describing autism by validating strengths more common among autistic people; identifying the individual aptitudes of autistic people and focusing on harnessing an individual's strengths, abilities and interests, recognising that autistic people have strengths, abilities, interests and/or expertise that often exceed their non-autistic peers. I explain how this can be done in Chapter 5.

While we should acknowledge that most autistic people (and their families) will face some difficulties, these difficulties should not define them. Neglecting autistic strengths and abilities will perpetuate misunderstanding and negativity around autism and limit outcomes. As I describe in Chapter 2, due to this general lack of understanding, autistic individuals all too often experience poor outcomes in education, employment and health. A strengths-based approach should also involve gathering, listening to and acting upon the voice of autistic individuals so we understand more about the experiences from autistic people themselves. I explain how this can be done in Chapter 3.

A different perspective

Autistic advocates are increasing sharing their personal accounts of living as an autistic person in a non-autistic world. These accounts will be unique in the same way that every non-autistic person's account would be. However, some experiences may be shared and autistic people may recognise that they have experiences in common which are generally not shared by non-autistic people.

Rather than considering autism as a medical disorder, we should be recognising it as one way of experiencing the world which is made difficult because the majority of the population are not experiencing the world in this way. An autistic person who engages in repetitive behaviours may be doing so in response to living in the non-autistic world. It may be helpful to consider how the autism neurotype (Wise, 2023) could be described by autistic people rather than diagnosed by a doctor. In this way, it may be helpful to consider anxiety, sensory and information gathering and processing, social interaction, friendships and relationships, expressive and receptive language development and the ability to assimilate specific and detailed information as a description of an autistic neurotype.

Incidentally, Attention Deficit Hyperactivity Disorder (ADHD) is a term which continues to be widely used. It may be helpful to use the term ADHers/ADers or ADH/AD neurotype, dependant on the type.

Identity-first or person-first language

Finally, I want to touch on how the language that we use reflects our changing understanding of autism. While some advocacy groups prefer person-first language, a person with autism, research has found that the majority of the autistic community prefer identity-first language, an autistic person.

Sinclair, (1999) could not be clearer in his declaration: 'I am not a person with autism. I am an autistic person.'

Sinclair explains that the term 'person with autism' suggests that the autism can be separated from the person. This is not the case. Autism is part of him and hard-wired into the way his brain works. He is autistic because he cannot be separated from how his autistic brain works.

Second, 'person with autism' suggests that autism is an unimportant part of the person's identity. However, Sinclair recognises that if he did not have an autistic brain, the person that he is would not exist. Autism is a fundamental feature of him as a person.

Third, 'person with autism' suggests that autism is something bad or to be ashamed of and should, therefore, be separated from the person. Sinclair, as many autistic individuals, advocates the use of identify-first language because he accepts and values himself as an autistic person.

Sainsbury (2009, p. 28) also objects to person-first language as 'we are not people who just happen to have autism; it is not an appendage that can be separated from who we are as people'.

Other autistic individuals share similar views on identity-first language with Wood: 'I don't use person first. I'm an autistic person … You wouldn't say there's a man with gayness' (Jon in Wood, 2019 p. 43).

'I am an autistic person. I reject the ideas of autism as an appendage or an 'add-on.' It isn't something that 'I have' and can leave behind if a choose to' (Kabie in Wood, 2019, p. 43).

However, the Autistic Self Advocacy Network (ASAN) also recognises that some parents of autistic children and young people, and some individuals themselves, prefer to use the term 'person with autism' because they do not consider autism to be key to their identity.

In line with the majority of autistic individuals and self-advocates, I use identify-first (lower case) language in this book. I use the same identity-first language when referring to individuals who are not autistic as non-autistic individuals. However, I also acknowledge personal preferences and will use person-first language when this is preferred. I also acknowledge that some individuals prefer to identify as Asperger's.

Reflections

On a scale of one to ten, how autism-affirming would your pupils rate your school?

Have you ever gathered the voice of your autistic pupils and asked them for their views, thoughts and feelings about school?

How many of your children may be diagnosed, undiagnosed, misdiagnosed and missed diagnosed as autistic?

How do your numbers of autistic pupils compare to published prevalence rates?

Are you aware of any members of staff who are or may be autistic?

Have you asked them what you can do to support them?

Summary

We are all responsible for ensuring that autistic children and young people are enabled to thrive as their autistic selves. It is, therefore, incumbent on us all to understand what this means for autistic and non-autistic children and young people alike, as we increasingly recognise the benefits associated with living in a neurodiverse world, which embraces the unique abilities of autistic individuals, among others. Understanding the views of autistic children and young people would be a positive first step to generating this understanding.

I have been gathering the views, thoughts and feelings of autistic pupils for many years. Around 50 children and young people have been kind enough to share their views, thoughts and feelings with me and I have conducted hundreds of interviews with them. Some of these children are now nearing the end of secondary school while others are relatively early in their primary school journey. The chapter concludes with the biographies of some of these amazing children and young people.

In this chapter, I have:

- Explained how the book came about.
- Highlighted that higher prevalence rates mean that we have an increasing number of autistic children and young people in our schools and that an increasing number of pupils are at risk of failure.
- Discussed autism and neurodiversity.
- Reflected on how autism is diagnosed and the shift to a strengths-based, identify-first approach.
- Concluded with the biographies of some of the children and young people who have contributed to this book.

Biographies of our contributors

'Will'

'Will' was one of the original contributors. He is the inspiration for this book after he told his teachers that the school was '100 per cent NOT autistic-friendly'. In 'Will's' own words: 'I am 13 years old, and I have autism and ADHD. I like games and computers. I go to secondary school with an SRP [specialist resourced provision] for autism. They have computers.'

Jack

Jack was one of the original contributors. He was born in 2010 and is an only child. He is lively and witty, kind with those he knows and shy with those he does not. He loves Marvel, comics, movies, trading cards, gaming and swimming. His autism/ADD-type behaviours were evident to professionals from nursery, though it took a further three years to get a formal diagnosis. He attended a mainstream primary from Reception to Year Three and then moved to a specialist unit attached to a mainstream primary school. Jack now attends a specialist secondary school with small class sizes and is thriving both personally and academically.

Toby

Toby started nursery in 2011. Not long into the autumn term, his nursery teacher noticed a number of traits indicating autism. Soon afterwards, Toby was diagnosed as autistic. He thrived in mainstream primary school and is doing well at secondary school, although he finds a number of subjects challenging. He is a hard worker and is a popular, confident, polite and kind member of his school community (and outside it too!). He does not receive any additional support at secondary school, although his handwriting is still poor. His sporting achievements would indicate that his gross motor skills are well honed! He is a sociable young man, though he will shy away from certain social situations where he feels uncomfortable, usually large group scenarios of adults, but is very comfortable in a large group of peers.

Eleanor

Eleanor was one of the original contributors. She has a wonderful sense of humour, and she is kind and loving. She lives with her dad (the source of her sense of humour) and her older sister. She loves adventure and has travelled as far as Australia with her dad and sister. Having left primary school, she moved to a specialist school for children with social communication differences. When she came back to visit recently, her teachers leapt for joy!

'Eric'

Also, one of the original contributors, I have known 'Eric' since he was six years old when he was in my Year One class. He is chatty and personable and on the mischievous side. He has two older sisters who love him to bits. He was always very interested in all things Doctor Who and would have liked everyone else to have been as interested as he was.

'David'

An original contributor, 'David' is shyly confident. He lives with his grandmother, siblings, aunties and uncles in a joy-filled, busy household. He moved to a special school for autistic children close to his home. They are lucky to have him.

'Alfie'

'Alfie' has a sunny disposition and never stops smiling from morning to night. He is creative and artistic and comfortable in his own skin. He moved to secondary school with a specialist resource provision for autistic pupils and I understand is going from strength to strength, fully involved in all aspects of school life.

'C'

'C' lives with his grandparent. Although he left many years ago, he is still in touch with his teachers. He was the founding member of a secondary school specialist resource provision, starting the year before it officially opened. I could not think of a better role model. Now studying 4 A Levels, he has grown up to be the handsome, intelligent young man he always told us he would be!

'Sophia'

'Sophia' has two brothers, one of whom is autistic. I realised she was autistic when she was in Year Six. A classic case of an intelligent, emotionally astute girl with strong social skills who was masking her difficulties and appearing to cope. The medical profession missed her autism completely – I hope things would be different today. 'Sophia' also moved to a school with a specialist resource provision and has thrived there. She is currently in the sixth form, studying A levels. What a joy to have her return recently for two weeks work experience.

'Lili'

I first interviewed 'Lili' in 2018. Highly intelligent and very clever, 'Lili' sees the world in pictures. I remember her astonishment when she realised that not everyone experienced the world in this way. She left our school to go to a mainstream secondary school, where I understand she is thriving. She is currently studying A Levels.

'Elias'

Elias was diagnosed at an early age. He found the environmental and social demands of primary school more difficult as he moved through the school. I have lost touch with his family, but I know that the transition to a mainstream secondary school was difficult for him.

Daniel

These are Daniel's own words.

> I am a rare child! I want to be an architect which I think I'll be really great at because I'm good at maths and art. Words that describe me are, apprehensive, gentle, kind, best brother ever, excellent worker. I'm really good at lots of things: science projects, designing things, football, Lego, crafts, drawing, comprehension and reading, gaming, maths and maths tests, art and my friendships. I'm a little worried about SATS but nothing else. I'd like to do more tests at home. I find these things tricky: listening, talking about my feelings, knowing if I upset people, knowing what not to say, talking about the right thing, being in crowds, arguments, playtimes and controlling my feelings sometimes. I find it harder to do my homework. I'm interested in cars, football, animals and flags. Being autistic means, I am one of the best in the class at maths. Oh, and I'm also best car owner ever.

Alex

These are Alex's own words.

> I am kind, lovely, funny, friendly, hardworking and calm. My strengths are electronic gaming, art, chess, swimming, using computers, making animations, maths, technology and Lego. I am good at gaming, maths, technology, Roblox, Minecraft and Fortnite. The things that are harder for me are: being in crowds, playtime, listening, eating in the lunch hall, talking to new people. My interests are Minecraft, Lego, Roblox, Rubik cube, cats, animals and cars.

Alex

In Alex's words.

> I live with my mum and sister who is 17 years old. I like going on my iPad and chilling in bed. I'm really good at drawing and maths. I don't really have any difficulties except getting to sleep at night. I look forward to going on the school bus and I enjoy maths because I'm so good at it. I would like to go to a maths club or a cooking club. I have a few friends; I like F the best. I like maths because I am so good at it and the worst is English because I find it hard to write. Three words to describe myself: sweet, energy, loving.'

Zayden

In Zayden's own words.

> I live with my mum and brother. I want to be a Red Arrows pilot. I am an inventor, fast, powerful, smart and I always have my aim on things. I am good at maths, making models, making animations, designing things, science, cookery, technology, electronic gaming, computers, tablets and reading train timetables. I find it harder to join in with games (this is number one), knowing what not to say (the most awkward for me), being in noisy places, crowds and assembly and talking about my feelings. My interests are cartoons, superheroes, Red Arrows, Saudi Falcons and science.

Mia

Mia said:

> I live with my mum, dad, brother and cat. I love maths, dancing, playing hide and seek and 'I spy with my little eye' in the car. My favourite food is chips, and my favourite colour is pink. I like glitter. My favourite [friend] is D. I like gymnastics, swimming and drawing. I find spellings, phonics and homework tricky. I think school is beautiful, nice and cute. I don't like homework expect maths. I go to drama club and tap-dancing class. My best friends are E (eight years old) and I. My friends are O, F and D. My favourite subjects are maths, art and music. My worst subject is English because we have to write sentences. It is so boring! Three words to describe myself: friendly, wise (may be not), beautiful and wonderful. I think that's four!

Blanka

In her own words:

> I live with my mummy, daddy and sister. We are Polish and speak Polish at home. My sister is called S and she is in Year 3; I am in Year 5. At home we like to play games together, especially Minecraft. I live in a flat and it is small. One day I would like to

live in a bigger house. My favourite food is Polish chicken – I just love it! My other favourite food is Chinese food. I have a lot of favourite colours. They are called 'cool' colours – blue, green, black and grey. My favourite animal is a cat. In Poland, my grandma has a grey cat called B. It's so funny because we always thought it was a she cat but last November we found out B was a he! I don't like sport, but I do like trampolining, climbing, swimming and table tennis. When I go to Holland, I play air hockey with my cousin. My best subject at school is D.and T. when we make things and a little bit of maths. I'm really good at art but not when I am distracted by people talking. I don't like noise when people look at me and I hate any type of dancing!

'Lena'

'Lena' said: 'I am good at reading, swimming, cycling, sport, maths and English. These things are harder for me: meeting and talking to new people, conversations and talking, talking about my feelings, when people move my things. My interests are space and archelogy.'

Scarlett

In Scarlett's words:

I live with my mum, baby brother and my birds. I love Anime. I am a nice friend, arty, generous, messy and a gamer. I am good at caring for animals, electronic gaming, art, science, drawing, using computers, designing things, crafts and drama. I find it harder to look at people, concentrate when people are talking, people moving my things, getting on with other people, conversations staying on topic.

'Yuen'

'Yuen' joined us in Year Five from Hong Kong. He made friends with other autistic pupils, although he did not know that they were autistic. He is good at maths and speaks excellent English. He is now in a local mainstream secondary school and I understand that he is doing well.

'Hanna'

'Hanna' was in Year Three when I first interviewed her. She lives at home with her parents. She has a wide number of friends and is generally able to advocate for herself and navigate the social demands of school.

'Orlaith'

Orlaith was in Year One when I first interviewed her. She lives at home with her parents and siblings. She has a supportive friendship group and is motivated to be like her friends. She is intelligent, friendly and inquisitive. She works extremely hard to hide her anxiety from adults and finds the transition into school and some parts of the school day difficult, at times. She knows more than most people about Harry Potter!

Rafa

My name is Rafa and I am 10. I live with my mummy and papi. I love coming to school. I have trouble understanding things and find learning at school hard but try to do my best. I got the gold tie prize this year. I really like my friends at school and after school clubs like running and football. I like going on school trips. I come to school by bus and train. I know a lot about trains and buses and am really good at remembering all the routes and stations. I'm great at cycling, swimming and climbing, and am learning how to ski. I'm happy most of the time but do not like small dogs and cats. I love going to Spain to visit my grandmother.

'Ivor'

'Ivor' moved from Hong Kong and has adjusted well to life in a British school. He can experience 'meltdowns' at school but is increasingly able to manage his self-regulation. He lives with his parents and older brother who is a great support to him.

Harri

Harri said:

> The Superloop [bus route] is very good but it's not the most important thing. My favourite thing is my mum, that's the most important thing. I am brave, helpful, sporty, kind, creative, talkative and honest. I like painting, crafts, gardening, working out bus and train routes, reading bus and train timetables, swimming, reading and chess. I don't like crowds, busy places and waiting. Sometimes I find it difficult to find friends to play with, knowing if I have upset people, knowing what not to say, meeting new people and listening. I want to be a paramedic and work at the hospital. It's a hard job but I'm sure I can do it. I also want to be a Gladiator and a firefighter.

James

In James's words:

> I have a very interesting family. My Great Grandfather is known for telling the future. I have four cousins called James because, in my family, we name the first child after the parents. I am cheerful and talkative of course, active (very!), creative, funny, friendly, sporty, loving and talkative. I have to admit I am a bit loud and a bit of a perfectionist. I am good at designing things, reading, chess, playing the drums, swimming, dance and painting. I do find some things difficult: listening, solving arguments, understanding personal space, knowing if I have upset people, accepting people's opinions, knowing what not to say, loosing and being in crowds. I want to be an architect and design a house for my mum.

Max

Figure 1.1 Max's biography.

References

American Psychiatric Association [APA]. (2013). *Diagnostic and Statistical Manual of Mental Disorders* (5th ed.). American Psychiatric Association.

Autistica. (2017). What is autism? www.autistica.org.uk/what-is-autism/what-is-autism

Baumer, N. and Frueh, J. (2021). *What Is Neurodiversity?* Harvard Health Publishing. Harvard Medical School.

BBC News. (6 May 2017). Rise in children in schools with autism spectrum disorder. www.bbc.co.uk/news/uk-wales-39796550

Centre for Disease Control and Prevention. (2023). Autism prevalence higher, according to data from 11 ADDM communities. CDC Newsroom. www.cdc.gov/media/releases/2023/p0323-autism.html

Coutinho, Claire MP, Minister for Children, Wellbeing and Families. (2023). Message to parents of children with SEND The Education Hub. Educationhub.blog.gov.uk. https://educationhub.blog.gov.uk/2023/03/02/children-with-send-claire-coutinho-minister-children-wellbeing-families/

Cunningham, M. (2020). 'This school is 100% not autistic friendly!' Listening to the voices of primary-aged autistic children to understand what an autistic friendly primary school should be like. *International Journal of Inclusive Education, 26*(12), 1–15. https://doi.org/10.1080/13603116.2020.1789767

Czech, H. (2018). Hans Asperger, national socialism, and 'race hygiene' in Nazi-era Vienna. *Molecular Autism, 9*(1). https://doi.org/10.1186/s13229-018-0208-6

Engelbrecht, N. (2021). Decoding autism in the DSM-5|Embrace autism. (n.d.). https://embrace-autism.com/decoding-autism-in-the-dsm-5

Huntley, M., Black, M., Jones, M., Falkmer, M., Lee, E., Tan, T., Picen, T., Thompson, M., New, M., Heasman, B., Smith, E., Bölte, S. and Girdler, S. (2019). *Action Briefing: Strengths-based Approaches*. Autism Research Group. Curtin University.

Kanner, L. (1943). Autistic disturbances of affective contact. *Nervous Child, 2*, 217-250.

Mehlmann-Wicks, J. (2020). Autism spectrum disorder. The British Medical Association. www.bma.org.uk/what-we-do/population-health/improving-the-health-of-specific-groups/autism-spectrum-disorder

National Autistic Society. (2022). The history of autism. www.autism.org.uk/advice-and-guidance/what-is-autism/the-history-of-autism

National Autistic Society. (2023). What is autism? Autism.org.uk; National Autistic Society. www.autism.org.uk/advice-and-guidance/what-is-autism

Prizant, B. and Fields-Meyer, T. (2022). *Uniquely Human: A Different Way of Seeing Autism*. Souvenir Press.

Russell, G., Stapley, S., Newlove-Delgado, T., Salmon, A., White, R., Warren, F., Pearson, A. and Ford, T. (2021). Time trends in autism diagnosis over 20 years: A UK population-based cohort study. *Journal of Child Psychology and Psychiatry, 63*(6), 674-682.

Sainsbury, C. (2009). *Martian in the Playground: Understanding the Schoolchild with Asperger's Syndrome*. Sage Publications Ltd.

Sandland, B. (2021). The spiral of self-identification of autism. Understanding self-identification of autism through firsthand experiences. The Department of Disability Inclusion and Special Needs, School of Education College of Social Sciences, University of Birmingham.

SEND Review: Right support Right place Right time A guide for children and young people to the special educational needs and disabilities (SEND) and alternative provision green paper. (2022). https://assets.publishing.service.gov.uk/media/6273e3dc8fa8f52075ac738d/SEND_green_paper_-_guide_for_children_and_young_people.pdf

Sinclair, J. (1999). Why I dislike 'person first' language: https://docs.google.com/document/d/12V4kRbz882q6UUeNbPB4ZxG8w8vfsxmSp2bMD2HpDQc/edit

Sinclair, J. (2013). Why I dislike 'person first' language. *Autonomy, the Critical Journal of Interdisciplinary Autism Studies, 1*(2), 2-3.

Wing, L. and Gould, J. (1979). Severe impairments of social interaction and associated abnormalities in children: Epidemiology and classification. *Journal of Autism and Developmental Disorders, 9*(1), 11-29.

Wise, S.J. (2024). *We're All Neurodiverse*. Jessica Kingsley Publishers.

Wolff, S. (1995). *Loners: The Life Path of Unusual Children*. Routledge.

Wood. R. (2019). *Inclusive Education for Autistic Children: Helping Children and Young People to Learn and Flourish in the Classroom*. Jessica Kingsley Publishers.

Chapter two

Why we must listen to autistic children and young people

Chapter outline

Fundamentally, we should seek to listen to the voices of our autistic pupils. First, it is our pupils' right as citizens to have their voices heard. Second, outcomes for our autistic pupils are poorer than their non-autistic peers. As I highlight throughout this chapter, generating a greater understanding of autism in general and of our autistic pupils specifically is necessary if we are to bring about change and improve outcomes for our pupils.

Historically, despite their right as citizens to have their voices heard, autistic children and young people have not been listened to. I question whether, despite best endeavours, any-thing much has changed. I include some personal perspectives of school, both historic and more up-to-date reflections, as a valuable insight to support our understanding of the impact on the lives of children who have not been listened to. I highlight that pupils continue to feel misunderstood at school and that they are requesting a greater understanding of autism from us, their teachers. I consider why autism may continue to be misunderstood. I stress that citizenship and human rights underpin everyone's right to be heard.

The outcomes for education, employment and health are poor for autistic children and young people. These poor outcomes can often be explained by a lack of understanding of autism in general, of individual needs specifically and of a failure to put in place the support that autistic children and young people need. These failures are often the result of a failure to gather, listen to and understand the perspectives of autistic children and young people.

Historically, children and young people have not been listened to

Historically, the views, thoughts and feelings of children with special educational needs, includ-ing those who may now be diagnosed as autistic, have been totally disregarded. Read and Walmsley (2006) re-formulated the meaning behind numerous historical, personal accounts of children with special educational needs to uncover their unwitting testimony of their school experience. This reveals a history of neglect and a disregard for the child's voice and often the child themselves. It highlights the necessity for us to gather and listen to our children's voices so that we can begin to understand the support which these children and young people need.

Armstrong (2003) set out to listen to children's stories to generate an understanding of how children experienced school. Armstrong spoke with 40 people of different ages who were educated in the mainstream and 'special' education systems between 1944 and 1994.

DOI: 10.4324/9781003396499-2

The history of autism serves to illustrate that it may be reasonable to assume that some of the individuals in Armstrong's study are (undiagnosed or misdiagnosed) autistic.

I include quotes from some of these individuals, so that their views, thoughts and feelings are recorded verbatim and not paraphrased through an adult. Their narrative serves as a powerful testimony to how they experienced a lack of understanding of themselves and explains why we need to begin to listen to our pupils. The accounts are all reflections of adults on their school experience, as their views as children and young people were not gathered at the time. The overwhelming narrative indicates that these children and young people felt powerless, as if their lives were directed and controlled externally as their voices were disregarded, ignored or overridden by (more) powerful adults.

The following quotes are reflections on not being listened to in school.

> You didn't get any choice at school. It used to be all about what the teacher wanted to do.
>
> *
>
> No one asked me.
>
> *
>
> Nothing was discussed with me.
>
> *
>
> They didn't bother asking you ... They just decide what's best for you without even bothering to ask you what you think.
>
> *
>
> They don't listen to the student's point of view and their suggestions.
>
> *
>
> Students should have rights to be able to be listened to. Just to be listened to and not to be fobbed off all the time.
>
> *
>
> If we were real students, we'd be given a choice of what we wanted.
>
> *
>
> [Other students] get listened to, they get their ideas or suggestions listened to, but we don't.
>
> (Armstrong, 2003, pp. 53, 59, 69, 72, 108, 109, 70, 110, respectively)

Critically, these individuals also requested a greater understanding of their world. Several of them felt that, if the support which they needed had been in place, they would have been successful in school. The failings of others left them with a feeling of unfairness and injustice which often stayed with them long into adulthood. The voice of autistic children was seldom heard as adults (however well intentioned) spoke for them or the child's voice was interpreted by a professional who may or may not know the child.

> We didn't get the chance to learn from them [our peers] and they didn't get the chance to like learn from us.
>
> *
>
> If they just try and put themselves in your shoes [they may understand how our needs can be met].
>
> (Armstrong, 2003, pp. 69, 72, respectively)

Policy and practice

I question whether, despite good intentions, our pupils would give a different, more positive narrative, of their experience of school and would feel that their views, thoughts and feelings are being taken into account so that the necessary support could be put in place. More up-to-date reporting would suggest not.

In 2002, the government published 'Autistic Spectrum Disorders: Good Practice Guidance' (Department of Education and Skills, Department of Health, 2002). One of the objectives was to involve autistic children and young people in decisions affecting their education.

However, the Autism Education Trust (AET) found that this was not happening consistently. In 2011, Charman et al. carried out a study on behalf of the AET to determine and advise on 'What is Good Practice in Autistic Education?' (Charman et al., 2011). This study sought to seek out, and identify, centres of excellence to develop a set of standards for the delivery of good practice in special schools, specialist autism schools and specialistic resourced provisions for autistic children and young people. The majority of the interviews were with teachers, parents and professionals, although 11 pupils, from one school, were interviewed. As the study found that 'there were [only] some notable examples of ensuring that pupils' voices were heard' there appears to be little evidence that the right of the child to be heard has disseminated into everyday practice in schools (Charman et al., 2011, p. 34; United Nations, 1989).

Analysis of the consultation responses to the Government SEND review: right support, right place, right time (March 2022) has been carried out. The consultation ran from March 2022 to July 2022 and received around 6,000 formal responses. The majority of responses were received from parents and carers (53.4 per cent of all respondents), followed by head-teachers/teachers/other teaching staff (18.4 per cent). There were 162 responses to the consultation from children and young people. This accounts for just 2.8 per cent of responses. Of these 162 responses, only 18 per cent were from primary-aged children and young people; just 29 responses!

We may not be enabling primary-aged children and young people to share their views, thoughts and feeling and ensure that their voices are heard.

Self-advocacy and personal perspectives as a valuable resource

Autistic individuals are increasingly communicating their own unique, personal, retrospective recounts of their experience of school. These accounts have the power to generate an understanding of how autistic children and young people have, and are, experiencing school, and in turn highlight the adaptations and adjustments which are necessary.

Sainsbury and Rowe have published personal recounts of their experiences of school as autistic individuals (Sainsbury, 2009; Rowe, 2013). Sainsbury recognises the importance of this as non-autistic people may have different assumptions about the school experience of their autistic pupils.

> In these debates, the voices of the people being discussed often go unheard [and] are rarely considered.
>
> (Sainsbury, 2009, p. 43)

> The real experts will usually be the autistic children.
>
> (Milton, 2014, p. 138, quoted in Wood)

Sainsbury attended a mainstream primary school. She records her own experiences of 'what a child with Asperger's syndrome is thinking, feeling and experiencing at school' in her book 'Martian in the Playground: Understanding the Schoolchild with Asperger's Syndrome' (Sainsbury, 2009, p. 21). Sainsbury provides a personal insight into what it is like to have Asperger's [autism] and offers her views, alongside the narratives of the school experiences of 25 children with Asperger's Syndrome. Sainsbury was about eight years old when she began to describe feeling different to other children. She did not receive a diagnosis until she was 20 years of age.

> I think that I might be an alien who has been put on this planet by mistake;
> I hope this is so, because this means that there might be other people in the universe like me.
>
> (Sainsbury, 2009, p. 25)

Alis Rowe also attended a mainstream primary school. She highlights that the people around her are totally oblivious to her everyday challenges as an autistic female. Her hope is that her book, *The Girl with the Curly Hair: Aspergers and me*, will build the bridge between autistic people and the rest of the world. She stresses that even her own family don't really know what it's like to be autistic, as autism can seem like an invisible condition. She also received her diagnosis as an adult.

Sainsbury feels 'regret and anger for the needless anger and pain' that school caused her and feels that if 'the right people had only been given the right information' her experience could have been different [better] (Sainsbury, 2009, p. 26). She believes that the mainstream classroom is very specifically designed to meet the needs of non-autistic children:

> It's not mainstream at all, but normalstream.
>
> (Sainsbury, 2009, p. 51)

> At the age of five or six I felt that my soul was dying.
>
> (Sainsbury, 2009, p. 86)

> I was in just about as much misery as any could have for most of my school years.
>
> (Sainsbury, 2009, p. 111)

> School was so traumatic for me that I was willing to do anything to get out of it.
>
> (Sainsbury, 2009, p. 111)

> I have very strong feelings of horror when I think of school.
>
> (Sainsbury, 2009, p. 86)

Sainsbury shares similarly negative experiences of school of other autistic people.

> It [school] was not worth all the misery I suffered.
>
> (Joliffe quoted in Sainsbury, 2009, p. 53)

> School was a torture ground in itself for me.
>
> ('Karen' in Sainsbury, 2009, p. 75)

Rowe recounts that:

> I used to run out of [primary] school because I did not want to stay.
>
> (Rowe, 2013, p. 25)

A note on Asperger's syndrome

Some people who received a diagnosis of Asperger's may continue to describe themselves using this terminology, usually because their diagnosis forms an important part of their identity, in a way that is not connected to official diagnostic terminology or to historical context. As highlighted in the previous chapter, others prefer not to use this term for the reasons stated in Chapter 1. I am respectful of individual preferences, which I acknowledge may alter over time.

As the number of autistic pupils continues to rise and school budgets are tightened (94 per cent of school leaders stated that they are finding it harder to resource the support required to meet the needs of pupils with SEND than they were two years ago, National Association of Headteachers) it will become increasingly important to engage autistic children and young people and use them as a valuable resource to facilitate an understanding of the support which they need.

Sainsbury believes that personal perspectives may be uniquely helpful in informing school practice (Sainsbury, 2000). She examines what being autistic means 'from the inside' recognising that 'All we need is understanding' (Sainsbury, 2009, p. 26). Rowe believes that most autistic people are able and willing to work and live a fulfilling life, with the right support and necessary adaptations and adjustments in place. The main problem is that most of us are unaware of what we need to do to help. A first step could be to gather, listen to and act upon the voice of our pupils.

This is important as it is increasingly accepted that these personal perspectives can provide a valuable source of information, explain the support that is needed and improve outcomes for autistic children and young people which, as I will highlight later in the chapter, are unnecessarily bleak across the education, employment and health sectors.

The right to be heard: citizenship and human rights

It is universally recognised that everyone has the right to be heard and that citizenship is dependent on active and meaningful participation in our own lives, including being involved in decisions which affect us. The Universal Declaration on Human Rights (1948), United Nations Convention on the Rights of the Child (1989), Convention on the Rights of Persons with Disabilities (2006), Children and Families Act (2014) and SEND Code of Practice (2015) all state that the child or young person has the right to be heard.

The Universal Declaration on Human Rights Article 2 (United Nations, 1948) states that:

> **Everyone** is entitled to **all** the rights and freedoms set forth in the declaration, so
> that fundamental human rights are **universally** protected. A citizen has **all** of the
> fundamental rights and freedoms granted to **all people**.

And Article 19:

> **Everyone** has the right to freedom of opinion and expression.

The fundamental right of children to be heard is also stated in the United Nations Convention on the Rights of the Child (United Nations, 1989) Article 12 1:

> Parties shall assure to the child who is capable of forming his or her own views **the right to express those views freely in all matters affecting the child**, the views of the child being given due weight in accordance with the age and maturity of the child.

Regardless of their cognition, language or means of communication, it is of utmost importance that the children and young people themselves are treated as the experts in their lives and we do everything that we can to listen to their voice. The recognition that all children have the right to be heard means we are all responsible for ensuring that all children are listened to.

The Convention on the Rights of Persons with Disabilities, Article 7, also specifies that individuals with disabilities should be enabled to be actively involved in decision-making processes which affect them (United Nations, 2006).

> 7.3 Parties shall ensure that children with disabilities have the right to express their views freely on all matters affecting them, their views being given **due weight** in accordance with their age and maturity, **on an equal basis with other children**, and to be provided with disability and age-appropriate assistance to realize that right.

If we need further evidence that we should be listening to the voices of all our pupils, I highlight the Children and Families Act (2014), which is an act to make provision about children, families and people with special educational needs or disabilities in the UK. In Chapter 6, Section 19, it states that a local authority **must have regard to the views, wishes and feelings of the child**; the importance of the child participating as fully as possible in decisions relating to the exercise of the function concerned; the importance of the child being provided with the information and support necessary to enable participation in these decisions and the need to support the child in order to facilitate the development of the child and to help them achieve the best possible educational and other outcomes.

The 2015 SEND Code of Practice takes on the guiding principles of the Children and Families Act, 2014, specifying what the principles mean in practice.

> 1.3 Local authorities **must** ensure that children, their parents and young people are involved in discussions and decisions about their individual support and about local provision.
> (Department for Education and Department of Health and Social Care, 2015)

It could not be clearer that all children and young people, including autistic children, must be given the opportunity to voice their views, thoughts and feelings, recognising that all children have a right to do so, and that these perspectives and experiences should be considered when determining policy and practice which affects them. Put simply, it is incumbent on us to provide the child or young person with the support necessary to enable participation in sharing their views, thoughts and feelings. We need to listen to these perspectives and take affirmative action in response to them.

To enable the active involvement and participation, of children and young people of all ages in decisions which affect them, it is necessary to engage them and find a way for them to participate in a meaningful way to share their views, thoughts and feelings. An approach which can be used to gather pupil voice is described in the next chapter.

Increasing numbers of autistic pupils in schools

The need to listen to autistic children and young people is becoming increasingly important, as the number of pupils identified as having 'special educational needs' continues to rise. Over one and a half million pupils in England have special educational needs (SEN). This is an increase of 87,000 from 2022 (Department for Education, 2023).

The number of autistic pupils in schools continues to rise in line with these numbers. There are currently over 180,000 autistic pupils in England. However, this is likely to be an underestimate as many families are waiting for substantial periods of time to receive a diagnosis for their child or young person, some families are choosing not to seek or pursue a diagnosis and children and young people may be missed and misdiagnosed.

Seventy-three per cent of autistic pupils are educated in mainstream schools and most believe that this is the right place for them. The Department for Education: SEND Review outlines government ambition for most children with SEND (including autistic children) to be educated in mainstream schools (Department for Education, 2022). The expectation is that the vast majority of autistic children and young people should be able to access the support they need to thrive in their local mainstream school.

However, due to a lack of understanding of autism from some teachers and other members of staff, pupils are often not accessing the support which they need to enable this. Autistic children and young people, and their families, were interviewed as part of the 2023 National Autistic Society School Report. They shared their experiences of school.

Three in four parents or carers (74 per cent) said that their child's school place did not fully meet their needs.

In 2017, this figure was four in ten.

The Autism Education Trust (2021) has stated its intention to drive towards improvement of outcomes for autistic children and young people. The Trust highlights in their 2021-2024 Improvement Plan that many schools are continuing to fail to make the necessary adaptations and adjustments to meet the needs of autistic pupils, despite their legal duty to do so.

As the Government's SEND review (2022) continues to advocate for an inclusive model of education, understanding the adjustments and adaptations which we need to make to support autistic children and young people should be a priority.

Autism training in schools

The Autism Education Trust (2021) is calling for enhanced autism training in all schools to develop a greater understanding of how to support staff working in schools, and other education establishments, to listen to autistic pupils to understand what they need. This could go some way to alleviating their feelings of being misunderstood by their teachers and other members of staff working to support them.

However, after autism was specifically referenced in the 2016 Initial Teacher Training Core Content Framework, it was removed in the 2019 Framework (Department for Education, 2019). Autism is, therefore, not referred to in the current Initial Teacher Training Core Content Framework.

This is because the Initial Teacher Training Core Content Framework is deliberately designed to emphasise the importance of high-quality or quality-first teaching. While it is understood that access to high-quality, whole-class teaching is important for all pupils, by not equipping trainee and early career teachers with learning on how to understand and support autistic pupils, and make the necessary adaptations and adjustments, the content specified in the framework may not be meeting the needs of autistic pupils.

Only 39 per cent of teachers surveyed by the National Autistic Society had received more than half a day's autism training.

The National Autistic Society (2023) has been monitoring autistic children and young people's views on our, their teachers', understanding of autism. Pupils continue to feel that we do not understand them as autistic pupils.

Seven in ten [autistic pupils] requested that their teachers understand more about autism.

This is consistent with findings from previous years.

Pupils report repeatedly that they feel that we, their teachers, do not understand about autism generally and about them as autistic pupils specifically. The support which is needed is not being offered and the necessary adaptations and adjustments are not being made as a result. If the Initial Teacher Training Core Content Framework were to provide an enhanced level of autism training, we may understand what we need to do to ensure that our autistic pupils are able to benefit from our high-quality, whole-class teaching.

The adaptations and adjustments which we need to make, to support our pupils, may be offered more readily if more were understood about autism. We may be surprised at how our autistic pupils are experiencing school and providing a tool to enable us to understand this may be helpful.

A lack of understanding of how autistic children and young people are experiencing the world, and school in particular, may be leading to unnecessarily high rates of absenteeism and exclusions, unsuccessful transitions to secondary school and poor outcomes in the higher education, employment and health sectors. Our pupils are also experiencing high levels of anxiety which they may be working hard to hide from us. These measures could all be improved by simply finding ways to listen to our autistic children and young people, understanding what they are communicating and acting upon their views, thoughts and feelings. I consider each of these factors in some detail as a way of illustrating why it is imperative that we begin to understand what we need to do to meet the needs of our pupils.

Academic outcomes

In 2022, the government published The SEND Review as a response to the widespread recognition that the SEND system is failing to deliver for children, young people and their families (Department for Education, 2022).

The report noted that too often the experiences and outcomes of children and young people (with SEN) are poor. The report notes that children and young people with SEND, including autistic children, are not consistently being helped to fulfil their potential. And that, **despite best endeavours**, mainstream schools and other providers are often ill-equipped to identify and support children and young people. Inconsistent practice makes this worse.

This results in poor academic outcomes for autistic pupils. In 2023, 20 per cent of pupils with SEN met the expected standard in reading, writing and maths (combined), compared with 59 per cent of pupils with no identified SEN (Department for Education, 2023). Of those pupils with SEN support, 24 per cent met the expected standard in reading, writing and maths (combined), while just 8 per cent of those pupils with an Education, Health and Care Plan met the combined expected standard. Many pupils with SEN support and EHC plans are autistic. The most common type of need among pupils with an EHC plan is autism. Almost one in three pupils with an EHCP are identified with a primary need of autism (116,000 pupils). The academic outcomes for autistic pupils continue to be significantly poorer than those of their non-autistic peers.

Absence and exclusions

It should come as no surprise that a high rate of school absence and exclusion is reported for autistic children and young people. Recent figures from the Department for Education (2022) show autistic children and young people are more than twice as likely to be excluded from school as pupils with no identified special educational need. Since 2011, the overall number of pupils excluded from school has risen by just 4 per cent with some regions seeing a drop in numbers. Over the same period of time, exclusions of autistic children and young people have increased by at least 44 per cent in every part of England.

Fifty-six per cent of parents of autistic children and young people reported that their child had been unlawfully sent home from school or denied an education and 30 per cent of autistic pupils were persistent absentees from school. Almost one third of parents reported that they had to give up their job due to their autistic child or young person being excluded from school (National Autistic Society, 2021).

Furthermore, over 10 per cent of parents responding to the National Autistic Society survey (2021) stated that their autistic child or young person had been suspended in the last two years and more than 20 per cent of parents said that their child had been informally excluded, at least once, in the same time period. Informal exclusions include children being asked not to come to school. Government figures show that the most common reason, at 22 per cent of fixed-term exclusions, for autistic children and young people being excluded is 'persistent disruptive behaviour' (Department for Education, 2022). Schools may sanction pupils for their behaviour rather than understanding it as a communication of a distressed and anxious, dysregulated child.

Dysregulated behaviour, which should be attributed to the communication of anxiety and stress, is often labelled as challenging or disruptive behaviour (challenging to whom?). If we lack an understanding of autism, we may treat behaviour by autistic pupils in the same way as we would treat the behaviour from our non-autistic pupils. This within-child view is extremely unhelpful and ultimately harmful to the child.

A lack of understanding of autism, together with a lack of understanding of the adaptations and adjustments that we should be making to meet the needs of our pupils, means that autistic pupils often end up on the receiving end of sanctions, negative consequences and ultimately poor outcomes. Misunderstanding of behaviours can, over time, lead to our pupils being at risk of getting stuck in a cycle of exclusion which can result in them being permanently excluded or moved to another school, where they are not known and more likely to be misunderstood.

With an improved understanding of autism, we may be able to develop an insight into the behaviours (communication) which our pupils may be exhibiting as a result of the complex interaction between the child, their environment and the people within the environment. As I highlight in Chapter 4, if we develop an insightful understanding of the cause of the behaviours, we can understand our part in the interaction and can make the necessary adaptations and adjustments to our practice to support the pupil's emotional regulation, sensory, social and environmental overload.

When teachers working in South Lincolnshire developed an enhanced understanding of their pupils, they witnessed an 80 per cent decline in permanent exclusions of autistic students between 2015 and 2019 (Autism Education Trust, 2020). This illustrates the importance of a whole-school approach to developing an enhanced understanding of autism so that the necessary adaptations and adjustments are understood by everyone working in the school. A whole-school approach recognises that understanding autistic children is the best approach to reducing exclusions.

Emotionally-based school avoidance (EBSA)

Autistic pupils can find navigating the sensory, social and environmental world of school confusing and stressful. Although our pupils may appear to be coping at school, they often experience high levels of stress and anxiety due to having to manage the non-autistic world. Some pupils are able to present their non-autistic selves and may appear to be managing the school day but if their (hidden) anxiety goes unrecognised, it may lead to them feeling overwhelmed and exhausted at the very thought of school. This can lead to emotionally based school avoidance (EBSA) and may ultimately result in poor mental health outcomes.

The term emotionally-based school avoidance recognises that this avoidance is the result of the sensory, social and environmental challenges which our pupils face. EBSA should not be considered as a deliberate act of defiance, but instead recognised as a complex issue which is inextricably linked with the stress and anxiety which the school day is causing. It is critical to understand why our pupils may be avoiding school and ask them what we can do to improve their experience of school. The adaptations and adjustments requested by our pupils and their families may limit or reduce emotionally based school avoidance.

Transitions

Families have reported that the transition from primary to secondary school is an incredibly difficult time for their autistic children and young people, and a lack of support at this time is one of their biggest challenges (National Autistic Society, 2023). The transition means a complete change to timetables, schedules and routines, as well as a daunting new sensory environment and increasingly challenging social situations. The primary school sharing the views, thoughts and feelings of the pupils with the secondary school may go some way to ensuring that the necessary adaptations and adjustments are put in place so that the pupils' needs can be met.

Education beyond school: higher education

It is estimated that around 2 per cent of the UK university population is diagnosed as autistic. However, autistic students are much less likely to start at university and complete their degree compared to their non-autistic peers. An investigation by the North-East Autism Society (NEAS) has found that, of those who started university in 2019, 36 per cent did not graduate with a degree (NEAS, 2023). The National Autistic Society (2023) reports cases where students have been excluded from college, and parents feel this is a result of their child's needs not being understood.

It is crucial that the needs of autistic university students are understood so that they are able to access the support which they need. An online questionnaire, to investigate the social and academic experiences of university, was completed by 26 autistic university students and 158 non-autistic students enrolled at UK universities. Although many strengths were reported regarding the academic skills of autistic university students, the students self-reported significant challenges and more mental health difficulties than their non-autistic peers. Their challenges focused on the social aspects of university life, including social skills, social support opportunities, and critically, poor levels of autism awareness from others.

The responses to open-ended questions indicate that autistic students feel there is a lack of awareness and acceptance of autism; that they have issues with self-advocacy and feel that they are grouped together as a homogeneous group as their individual strengths and difficulties are misunderstood. In line with primary and secondary school pupils, university students also request that they are better understood and highlight the need for more support.

Employment

The Office for National Statistics (ONS) published data in 2021 which highlights that just 29 per cent of autistic adults are in any kind of employment compared to around 80 per cent of the population as a whole. Only 16 per cent of autistic adults are currently in full-time paid employment and only 15 per cent of autistic young people believe that employers will offer them a job.

The Ambitious About Autism report stated that 72 per cent of employers say they have not built neurodiversity into their inclusion policies and do not understand neurodiversity. Therefore, too few neurodivergent individuals (including autistic individuals) are managing to find employment and thrive in the workplace. The estimated cost to society, as a result of the lack of support for autistic people and their families, is £32bn per year. This is more than the cost of stroke, cancer and heart disease combined (Autism Education Trust, 2021).

To support more autistic people joining the workforce, and address this disparity in employment rates, there are a variety of measures that could be taken.

The National Autistic Society runs an Autism at Work programme to increase the number of autistic people in paid employment by generating an understanding of autism and making employers aware of autistic talent and the benefits of having a neurodiverse workforce.

The more employers understand about how they can support autistic employees, the more they will benefit from the many strengths which autistic people offer.

Health outcomes

Health outcomes for autistic people are also poor. The life expectancy gap for autistic individuals is approximately 16 years, on average, compared to the general population. As I highlight, autistic children and young people carry high levels of stress and anxiety which, over time, may lead to poor mental health outcomes. Almost 80 per cent of autistic adults experience mental health problems during their lifetime (Department of Health and Social Care, 2021). Mind reports that although autism is not a mental health problem, autistic people may be more likely to experience poor mental health and have a mental health problem like depression or anxiety at some time in their lives (Mind, 2022).

Many of the reasons for poor health outcomes are due to not taking the time to listen to patients and a general lack of understanding of autism, perhaps surprising amongst medical practitioners. This lack of understanding can result in autistic children and young people being more likely to experience negative attitudes from non-autistic people, who may not understand or accept the challenges which they face. There are also challenges associated with interacting with, and living in, a non-autistic world, which may not meet the child or young person's sensory, social, language or communication needs. As a result, autistic children and young people may be more likely to experience stigma and discrimination.

Missed and misdiagnosis can also be barriers to support as some experiences of autism may overlap with symptoms of poor mental health. This may mean that experiences of autism are mistaken for mental health problems which may make it harder to get the right support which, in turn, can contribute to stress, anxiety and depression. It can be difficult to get the right support, both for autism and for mental health. It can take a long time (many years) to get an autism diagnosis.

The mental health and wellbeing of autistic children and young people could be improved with an increased understanding of autism amongst health workers and the population as a whole.

Reflections

How do pupils' historical accounts of school compare to our pupils' experience of school today?

Would our pupils tell us that they feel listened to and understood by everyone that they come into contact with at school and that the adaptations and adjustments which they need are in place?

Are our pupils aware of their rights as citizens?

Have all members of staff engaged in training to generate a greater understanding of autism? Was the voice of our autistic pupils part of this training?

How many of our pupils would request that their teachers have a greater understanding of autism?

Do the outcomes of our autistic pupils compare favourably with those of our non-autistic pupils?

Summary

This chapter highlights the (unnecessarily) poor outcomes for autistic children and young people in many areas of their lives. I highlight powerful historic accounts of how autistic pupils have experienced school and, despite best endeavours, question how much has changed. I highlight that, although everyone has the right to be heard, the views, thoughts and feelings of autistic children and young people are not being sought, resulting in a misunderstanding of what they need. I have catalogued negative experiences, where autistic behaviour is often misunderstood, and autistic voice is not being sought.

Autistic children and young people are being unintentionally let down. This often starts at school where there may be a lack of understanding of autism amongst some teachers and other members of school staff. Teaching about autism, and how to understand autistic pupils, so that their needs can be met, is no longer mandated on Initial Teacher Training programmes and Early Career Frameworks for teachers. This may result in autistic communication and interactions being misunderstood, resulting in the child or young person being excluded by school staff or 'self-excluding' themselves as they are unable to cope in a non-autistic environment that has not been adapted to meet their needs. As the secondary school environment is typically a more challenging environment for autistic children and young people, outcomes are unlikely to improve as the pupil transitions to secondary school.

Autistic young people are understandably pessimistic about their employment opportunities. The lower progression rates of autistic young people into higher education mean that they are disadvantaged in the jobs market, with only 16 per cent of autistic adults currently in full-time, paid employment. This results in an unnecessary waste of resource. Higher levels of engagement with autistic individuals could lead to an improved understanding of how simple adaptations and adjustments could support autistic individuals in the workplace.

Even within the health sector, autism is misunderstood, resulting in poor outcomes for physical and mental health and wellbeing. Again, a greater understanding of autism could lead to an improved understanding of how simple adaptations and adjustments could support autistic individuals in the health sector.

As the number of autism diagnoses continues to rise, an increasing number of children and young people are being, unintentionally, failed across multiple sectors. This is, all too often, due to adults not listening to, and acting upon, the voices of autistic children and young people which, in turn, leads to a lack of understanding of autism and a failure to understand how to support them.

Listening to, and acting upon, the voice of autistic children and young people could, and should, lead to improved outcomes and enable them to make a valuable contribution to a neurodiverse society.

In this chapter, I have highlighted:

- How insider views and personal perspectives can be used to generate an understanding of autism generally and the needs of autistic children and young people specifically.
- The right to be heard is everyone's right as citizens and is universally recognised.
- Evidence that a lack of understanding about autism, and the support which autistic children and young people need, is resulting in unnecessarily poor outcomes for them across the education, employment and health sectors.

References

Armstrong, D. (2003). *Experiences of Special Education: Re-Evaluating Policy and Practice through Life Stories*. Routledge Falmer.

Autism Education Trust. (2020). Exclusions. www.autismeducationtrust.org.uk/exclusions

Autism Education Trust. (2021). 2021-2024 Improvement Plan. www.autismeducationtrust.org.uk/sites/default/files/2021-09/AET_Strategy_Summary_2021-24.pdf

Charman, T., Pellicano, L., Peacey, L., Peacey, N., Forward, K. and Dockrell, J. (2011) What is good practice in autism education? Centre for Research in Autism and Education (CRAE), Department of Psychology and Human Development, Institute of Education, University of London. Autism Education Trust. Available at: https://research-management.mq.edu.au/ws/portalfiles/portal/83300571/82950951.pdf

Department of Education and Skills, Department of Health. (2002). *Autistic spectrum disorders: Good practice guidance*. DfES Publications.

Department for Education. (2011). Support and aspiration: A new approach to special educational needs and disability. The Stationery Office Limited. www.educationengland.org.uk/documents/pdfs/2011-green-paper-sen.pdf

Department for Education. (2015). SEND Code of practice: 0 to 25 Years. www.gov.uk/government/publications/send-code-of-practice-0-to-25

Department for Education (2019) Initial teacher training core content framework. Department for Education. https://assets.publishing.service.gov.uk/media/6061eb9cd3bf7f5cde260984/ITT_core_content_framework_.pdf

Department for Education. (2022). SEND review: Right support, right place, right time. www.gov.uk/government/consultations/send-review-right-support-right-place-right-time

Department for Education. (2023a). Statistics: Special Educational Needs (SEN). www.gov.uk/government/collections/statistics-special-educational-needs-sen

Department for Education (2023b). https://explore-education-statistics.service.gov.uk/find-statistics/special-educational-needs-in-england

Department of Health and Social Care. (2021). New landmark strategy to improve the lives of autistic people. www.gov.uk/government/news/new-landmark-strategy-to-improve-the-lives-of-autistic-people

Gov.uk. (2014). Children and Families Act 2014. www.legislation.gov.uk/ukpga/2014/6/contents/enacted

Lundy, L. (2007). Voice is not enough: Conceptualising Article 12 of the UN Rights of the Child. *British Education Research Journal*, 33(6), 927–942.

Milton in Wood, R. (2019). *Inclusive Education for Autistic Children: Helping Children and Young People to Learn and Flourish in the Classroom*. Jessica Kingsley Publishers.

Mind. (2022). Autism and mental health. www.mind.org.uk/about-us/our-policy-work/equality-and-human-rights/autism-and-mental-health/

National Autistic Society. (2017). All Party Parliamentary Group on Autism, Autism and education in England.

National Autistic Society. (2021). School Report 2021. www.autism.org.uk/what-we-do/news/school-report-2021

National Autistic Society. (2023). National Autistic Society Education Report. www.autism.org.uk/what-we-do/news/education-report-2023

North East Autism Society (2023) Autistic students most likely to drop out of university: Investigation. www.ne-as.org.uk/news/autistic-students-most-likely-to-drop-out-of-university-investigation

Office for National Statistics (ONS). (2022). Outcomes for disabled people in the UK – Office for National Statistics. www.ons.gov.uk/peoplepopulationandcommunity/healthandsocialcare/disability/articles/outcomesfordisabled

Read, J. and Walmsley, J. (2006). Historical perspectives on special education, 1890-1970. *Disability and Society*, 21(5), 455–469.

Rowe, A. (2013). *The Girl with the Curly Hair*. Lonely Mind Books.

Sainsbury, C. (2009). *Martian in the Playground: Understanding the Schoolchild with Asperger's Syndrome*. Sage Publications Ltd.

UNICEF. (2016). UN Convention on the Rights of the Child (UNCRC) – UNICEF UK. www.unicef.org.uk/what-we-do/un-convention-child-rights

United Nations. (1948). Universal Declaration of Human Rights. United Nations. www.un.org/en/about-us/universal-declaration-of-human-rights

United Nations. (1989). The United Nations Convention on the Rights of the Child. www.unicef.org.uk/what-we-do/un-convention-child-rights

United Nations. (2006). United nations convention on the rights of persons with disabilities. www.un.org/disabilities/documents/convention/convention_accessible_pdf.pdf

Chapter three

The three houses approach to gathering pupil voice

Chapter outline

In this chapter, I explain the three houses approach; how to use the approach to gather pupil voice in semi-structured group and individual interviews and how the approach can be adapted to meet the individual needs of children and young people, recognising that each child is unique. I discuss the benefits of the semi-structured interview format and explain the origin of the three houses approach.

I highlight how the three houses can be used to identify topics (things about school) which the pupils identify as being important to them. I introduce the child-initiated topics which were uncovered using the three houses approach and highlight the three key themes which emerged. These themes may help us to understand what we need to change about our schools to ensure that they are autism-affirming from the pupils' perspective. Further implications for practice are discussed in subsequent chapters.

The aims of the three houses approach

The three houses approach can be used to gather the views of our autistic pupils. Accounts of their lived experiences of school could be a valuable resource in helping us to generate an understanding of how our pupils are experiencing school. Our pupils' unique perspectives should help us to understand what we need to change to ensure that our pupils have a positive school experience.

I was prompted to find out more about how our pupils were experiencing school after a pupil expressed his view that our school was not doing enough to meet his needs as an autistic pupil. In fact, he burst into the staff room and declared that the school was '100% NOT autistic-friendly'! I recognised that we had little understanding of our autistic pupils' perspectives of school. We needed to understand how they were experiencing the school, what was important to them, what was going well, what was not going well and what we needed to change to improve their experience of school and ensure that they felt empowered in decisions which affect them, specifically what an autism-affirming school should be like.

When I reflected on how to gather the views, thoughts and feelings of our pupils, I wanted an approach which would support the pupils in generating topics, things about the school, which they felt were important. I did not want a (non-autistic) adult to decide the things about

DOI: 10.4324/9781003396499-3

the school which were impacting on the pupils' school experience. It was also important that the approach encouraged collaboration and discussion on these child-initiated topics, appropriate to the language, age and maturity of the pupils, to generate an understanding of what was going well in school, what was not going well and what we needed to change in school, from our pupils' perspective. The three houses approach enables the pupils to generate topics which are important to them, to share their views on each of these topics so that we can generate an understanding of the adaptations and adjustments which we need to make to create autism-affirming schools from our pupils' perspective.

Teachers' Toolbox

In subsequent chapters, I introduce a teachers' toolbox of practical and helpful resources which may be helpful for us, as teachers.

An introduction to the three houses approach

The three houses (Turnell and Edwards, 1999; Weld, 2008) approach is a simple tool which can be used to support our pupils in generating topics, things about the school, which are important to the pupils themselves, and gather their views, thoughts and feelings on each of these topics in turn. Essentially, the approach uses a visual framework (Figures 3.1 and 3.2) and a simple interview script (Appendix 1) to enable the pupils to share their perspectives of school by asking them what is going well and what is not going well on each of the topics, which are impacting them, in turn. It also uncovers the pupils' perspectives on what we need to change in school to enable them to have positive school experiences.

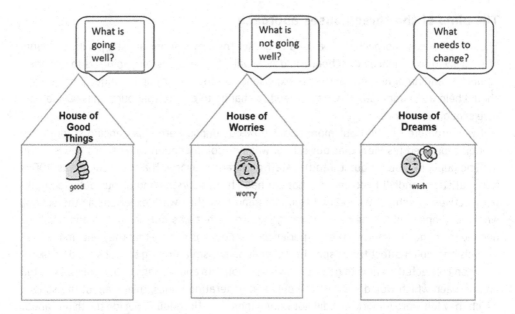

Figure 3.1 The three houses visual.

Adapted by the author from Turnell, A. and Edwards, S. (1999); Weld, D. (2008). Widgit Symbols © Widgit Software Ltd 2002–2024 www.widgit.com

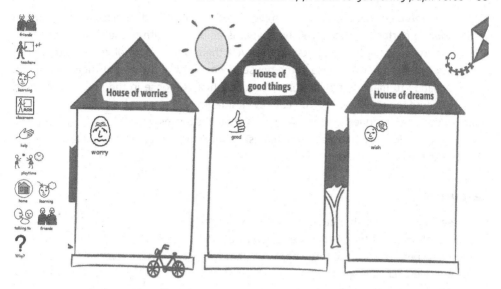

Figure 3.2 The three houses visual.

Adapted by the author from Turnell, A. and Edwards, S. (1999); Weld, D. (2008). Widgit Symbols © Widgit Software Ltd 2002–2024 www.widgit.com

In brief, the three houses approach may be used to gather pupil voice, as follows:

Stage 1. Invite your pupils to take part in a small group interview or group discussion. Introduce the three houses visual tool (Figures 3.1 and 3.2) and begin to ask the pupils about their experience of school by asking them three questions:

> What is going well at school?
> What is not going well at school?
> What do we need to change at school?

> Record the pupils' responses to each of these questions within the three houses visual framework. Record what is going well at school within the house of good things; what is not going well within the house of worries; and what we need to change within the house of dreams. The pupils' responses will highlight topics, things about the school, which are important to them. Topics that are assigned to the house of good things are having a positive impact on their school experience. Topics that are assigned to the house of worries are having a negative impact on their experience of school. Topics which are placed in the house of dreams are things about the school that we need to change. Record the discussion so you can go back to it later.

Stage 2. Invite your pupils to take part in an individual interview. Use the three houses visual tool and the interview script to ask the pupils about each of the topics, which they raised in the group interviews. This ensures that we are asking the pupils about topics which are important to them. Use the interview script to ask the pupils the same three questions about each of the topics in turn and write down their responses in the three houses visual. For example, if your pupils raised friends as a topic which was important to them, ask them what is going well with friends and record their response in the house of good things. Ask them what is not going well with friends and record their response in the house of worries. Ask them what their friends can change to make things better and record their response in the house of dreams. Record the discussion so you can revisit it later.

Stage 3. After the interviews, show the pupils their responses which have been recorded within the three houses visual and ask them if there is anything which they would like to add, change or remove.

Resources

The three houses approach requires minimal resources.

A visual of the three houses (Figures 3.1 and 3.2).

Paper and pens to draw the three houses with the pupils, if this is preferred.

The interview script (Appendix 1).

Visuals of the topics which your pupils raised in the group interviews.

A visual timer, such as a sand timer.

A device to record the interview.

Two examples of the three houses visual tool are illustrated below. These can be printed before you meet with the pupils or drawn with them at the start of the interview.

The topics which the pupils raised

The three houses approach can be used to discover the topics, things about the school, which are important to our pupils; things which are having a positive or negative impact on their school experience. You may be able to quickly discover the topics which are important to your pupils by asking them the three open questions: What is going well? What is not going well? and What do we need to change at school?

The topics which our pupils raise help us to generate an understanding of how our pupils are experiencing school, the elements of the school experience which are successful or particularly challenging for them and the adaptations and adjustments which we need to make to improve their experience of school.

When using the three houses approach in small group interviews, our pupils highlighted the following eight topics which were impacting on their experience of school, positively or negatively. These topics were:

- Teachers
- Friends and peers
- Lessons and learning
- Classroom environment
- Breaktime and lunchtime
- People who help me
- Home learning/homework
- Arriving and leaving school

These topics were all child-initiated and this is important. The pupils recognised that each of these topics was having a positive or negative effect on their experience of school. I wonder whether your pupils would raise similar topics.

Using the pupils' responses to develop themes and sub-themes

It may be helpful to analyse our pupils' responses (qualitive data) to determine themes and sub-themes. This may give further insight into how our pupils are experiencing school and support our understanding of the changes which we need to make to ensure a positive school experience. Themes, here, can best be described as repeated patterns of meaning (Braun and Clarke, 2006). It may be helpful to consider themes as a way of summarising what the pupils are really telling us about their experience of school. You may find it helpful to follow these steps when analysing your pupils' responses.

Step 1   Begin by familiarising yourself with your pupils' responses to the three questions, what is going well, what is not going well and what do we need to change in school. Do this by looking at what you or your pupils have written in the three houses and by listening to the recordings of the interviews. Note down your initial ideas on any emergent themes.

Step 2   Notice any aspects which are of interest and highlight (code) these so themes can begin to be identified. This may be words or phrases which are repeated within the three houses or within the interview recordings. Highlight any word or phrase which is repeated in a specific colour. For example, every time a pupil mentioned anything to do with anxiety, stress or worry, highlight these words or phrases in one colour. Continue to sort words and phrases which you have highlighted into potential themes and collate all the relevant responses into these themes.

Step 3   You should be able to identify themes which are emerging through this process. Define and name each of the key themes and the identify any sub-themes. Remember that themes can be considered as repeated patterns of meaning. Sub-themes are 'underneath' each key theme, focus on different elements of the overarching theme and support our understanding of the theme. For example, anxiety may emerge as an overall theme. The parts of the experience that were causing anxiety may be considered as sub-themes.

Step 4   If possible, take the themes back to the pupils to ensure that the themes make sense to the pupils. The pupils usually enjoy this part of the process.

If you are interested in reading more on how to analyse your pupils' responses, this stepped approach to thematic data analysis was devised by Braun and Clarke (2006) and is used widely when analysing qualitative data.

Themes and sub-themes

When I analysed the responses from the hundreds of interviews my colleagues and I carried out, three key themes emerged. A number of sub-themes, which are illustrated in Figure 3.3, emerged 'underneath' each of the themes. Each of these themes and sub-themes have implications for practice and will be discussed in subsequent chapters. I suspect that you may find

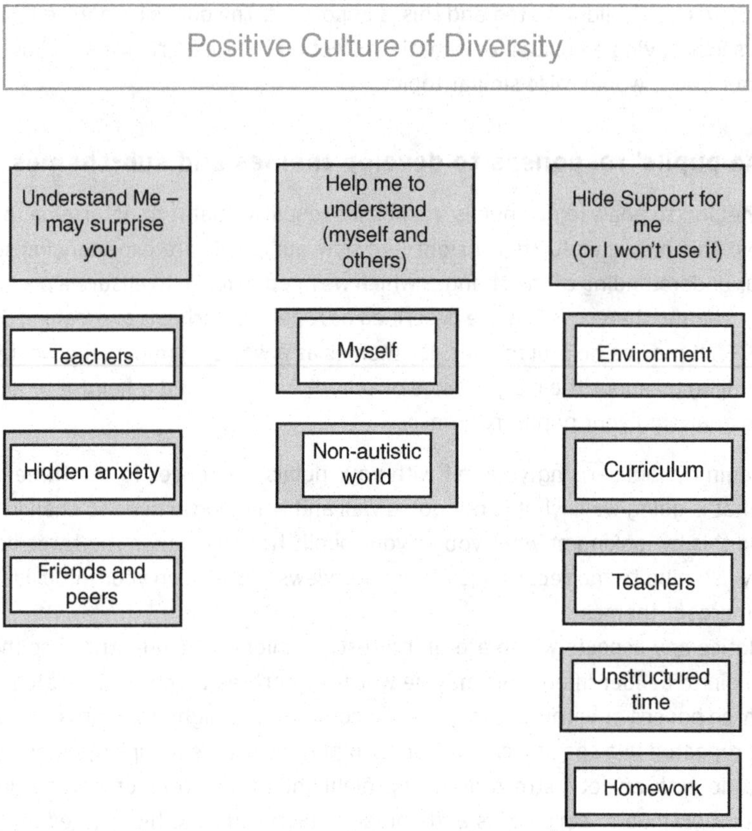

Positive Culture of Diversity

Understand Me – I may surprise you	Help me to understand (myself and others)	Hide Support for me (or I won't use it)
Teachers	Myself	Environment
Hidden anxiety	Non-autistic world	Curriculum
Friends and peers		Teachers
		Unstructured time
		Homework

Figure 3.3 A visual representation of the themes and sub-themes.

that similar themes emerge in your school. Equally, you may discover themes that are unique to your pupils or to your setting.

Three key themes emerged:

Understand me – I may surprise you.
Help me to understand – understand myself and understand others.
Hide support for me – or I won't use it.

Pupils were clear that, when creating autism-affirming schools, we need to adopt a whole-school approach, which I have described as a positive culture of diversity. A number of sub-themes lie underneath each overarching theme.

Several other studies have also explored the experiences of autistic pupils. These studies primarily explore the experiences of post-primary pupils, however, the pupils have experiences in common with primary-aged pupils and similar themes and sub-themes emerge. The bold print indicates themes and sub-themes which the older pupils have in common with our primary-aged pupils. As I have already discussed, there is a lack of literature on pupil voice and we need to begin to explore the perspectives of our pupils, if we are to generate an understanding of their perspectives of school and create autism-affirming schools from their perspective.

Saggers, Hwang and Mercer (2011) explored the experience of nine autistic pupils (seven boys and two girls), aged 13 to 19. The pupils, who had all been diagnosed as autistic, all met the requirements for additional government-funded education support. The students were enrolled in a large mainstream high school in Brisbane, Australia. They identified the following six themes and sub-themes which were discovered through semi-structured interviews with the pupils.

These were:

- **Teacher characteristics - positive and negative**.
- **Curriculum-related issues - workload; assessment; demand for handwriting; technology**.
- **Support mechanisms - attitudes to specialist support; types of support, delivery of support**.
- **Friendships - perceptions towards friends and friendships; attitudes towards socialising**.
- **Environmental considerations - crowds; noise**.
- Teasing and bullying.

Similarly, Goodall (2018, 2020) used various methods to gather the views of 12 autistic pupils, aged 11 to 17, specifically about their views on how they were experiencing a mainstream secondary school.

He identified the following three themes and a number of sub-themes:

- **Exclusion in inclusion - feelings of dread and isolation; feeling misunderstood; feeling unsupported**;
- **Supporting me - Supportive teachers; supportive curricula; supportive environments**;
- Inclusion and me - defining inclusion; **autism and mainstream inclusion**.

Humphrey and Lewis (2008) interviewed a total of 20 pupils aged 11 to 17 years of age. These pupils were drawn from the four chosen mainstream secondary schools in the north-west of England. They also identified similar themes.

The themes which they identified were:

- **Characteristics associated with autism**
- **Constructing an understanding of autism**
- **Anxiety and stress in school**
- **Relationships with peers**
- **Negotiating difference**
- **Working with teachers and other staff**

When Horgan, Kenny and Flynn (2023) carried out a systematic review of the experiences of pupils in mainstream post-primary education, they also uncovered similar themes and sub-themes.

- **Demands of mainstream - academic inclusion; sensory environment; transitions**;
- **Social participation - relationships with peers; relationships with teachers and support staff**; bullying;
- **Impact on the pupil - wellbeing and mental-health; autistic identity**.

The eight topics raised by our pupils have been raised by pupils in other studies. We can, therefore, have some confidence that these topics are important to many autistic pupils, and are not unique to the pupils in one primary school. This knowledge may be helpful in generating an understanding of our pupils' perspective of school. It may help us to understand the elements of the school experience which are impacting, positively and negatively, on their experience of school and help us to understand more about how we can create autism-affirming schools from our pupils' perspectives.

Reflections on the three houses approach

How to determine which pupils to interview

Determine a set of criteria which the pupils (participants) should meet. I interviewed pupils in Year 1 to Year 7 who had been diagnosed as autistic or were on the social communication pathway and were likely to receive a diagnosis of autism. Most of the pupils communicated verbally and some used non-verbal means of communication. All of the pupils I interviewed identified as male or female and I interviewed a similar number of girls and boys. I interviewed each of the pupils on several occasions.

Topics raised by the pupils

As I highlighted in Chapter 1, autistic pupils have been given little opportunity to have their voices heard and non-autistic adults have often selected the topics which they thought were important to the pupils. This may mean that the adults have been unwittingly failing to consider what is important to the pupils themselves. Furthermore, as the focus may have been to seek the child's perspective, we may have missed the opportunity to use pupil voice as a powerful catalyst for change and improvement (Harrington et al., 2014).

By using the three houses approach, it may be possible to enable our pupils to determine the topics that are important to them. We can then begin to react positively to our pupils' views and understand the adaptations and adjustments which we need to make to enable a more positive school experience for them. I find the three houses approach to be a fun and engaging tool in both group and individual interviews. It involves the pupils, enables their meaningful participation and enables them to share their views, thoughts and feelings of school.

As I have explained, group interviews can be used to actively engage the pupils and give them the opportunity to initiate topics which are important to them. This is important, as it enables the pupils to highlight topics which they want to talk about. The topics may be unique to a pupil or school or raised by several pupils. It is important not to be presumptuous about what is important to the pupils, especially if we are not autistic ourselves and, therefore, do not share the experiences of the school in the same way as our autistic pupils.

Generating a greater understanding linked to the pupils' understanding of themselves as autistic children and young people is requested by the pupils. This may give us confidence that the themes of understand me – I may surprise you and help me to understand – understand myself and understand others are significant. Pupils request that they are supported to understand themselves as autistic children and young people and they ask that non-autistic people develop an understanding of their autistic world. By generating a greater understanding, we may be better equipped to offer the support which the pupils need. The theme of requesting support with several different aspects of school is also requested by a large number of pupils. This may give us confidence that the theme, of hide support for me - or I won't use it, is also significant.

How to use the three houses approach to gather pupil voice in group and individual interviews

Group interviews

As I have highlighted, the three houses approach can be used in group interviews to uncover the topics and things about the school which are important to our pupils and are impacting on them, positively or negatively. When organising group interviews, it may be helpful to organise your pupils into year groups or with pupils who are similar in age. Quickly establish some ground rules for the interview to ensure that the more articulate pupils do not dominate the group. During the group interviews, you may find it helpful to sit the pupils in a semi-circle around a table or on the floor (Keats, 2000; Kvale, 2007).

Begin by drawing a simple outline of three houses in front of the pupils; do not explain why you have done this at this stage. Label the three houses which you have drawn: the house of good things; the house of worries and the house of dreams. For most groups of pupils, it will be helpful to include visual symbols; use a smiley face (or thumbs up) beside the label in the house of good things; a sad face (or thumbs down) in the house of worries; and a dream symbol in the house of dreams (Figures 3.1 and 3.2). Alternatively, print the three houses visual and present this to the pupils.

Begin by asking your pupils to share their views on what is going well at school. It is important to start with what is going well for the pupils as this helps them to feel comfortable with the process. Your pupils' responses to this question should be recorded in the house of good things. The pupils are subsequently asked to respond to the question what is not going well and what they would like us to change about the school. Your pupils' responses are recorded respectively in the house of worries and the house of dreams. The house of dreams is important when considering the adaptations and adjustments which we need to make in the school.

During the group interviews, you may begin to develop an initial understanding of your pupils' perspectives of school as you use the three houses approach to engage them in an initial discussion about their experience of school. However, I am mindful that asking a group of pupils an open question about their perspective of school can lead to a period of silent reflection or the rather unhelpful response 'I don't know'. In this case, it may be helpful to ask your pupils to reflect on each, or some, of the eight topics highlighted below:

Teachers
Friends and peers
Lessons and learning
Classroom environment
Break time and lunch time
People who help me.
Home learning/homework
Arriving and leaving school

You could end the interview with three open questions about the school: What is going well? What is not going well? and What do we need to change? Your pupils may be more able to think about topics which are important to them at the end of the group interview.

Individual interviews

Following the group interviews, invite each of the pupils, who took part in the group interviews, to an individual interview. The individual interviews facilitate further discussion on each of the topics raised in the group interviews, and also enable your pupils to raise any topics which are important to them but may not have been raised previously. The pupils are invited to share their views on each of the topics which they raised in the group interviews. Use the interview scrip (Appendix 1) and ask them what is going well, what is not going well and what we need to change about each topic in turn. As in the group interviews, the pupils' responses are recorded respectively in the three houses. Record the interview so that you can capture the full narrative (Figures 3.4 to 3.9).

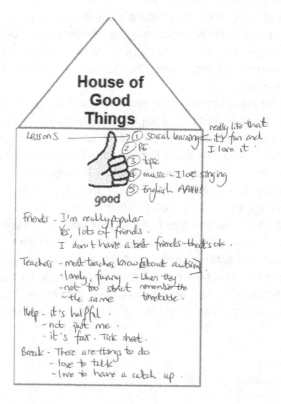

Figure 3.4 An example of the house of good things, completed in an individual interview.

Widgit Symbols © Widgit Software Ltd 2002–2024 www.widgit.com

Figure 3.5 An example of the house of good things, completed in an individual interview.

Widgit Symbols © Widgit Software Ltd 2002-2024 www.widgit.com

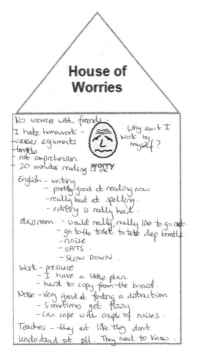

Figure 3.6 An example of the house of worries, completed in an individual interview.

Widgit Symbols © Widgit Software Ltd 2002-2024 www.widgit.com

Figure 3.7 An example of the house of worries, completed in an individual interview.

Figure 3.8 An example of the house of dreams, completed in an individual interview.

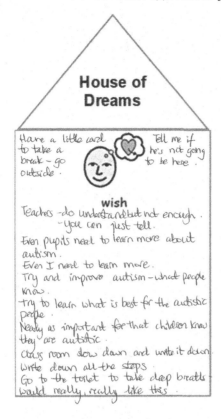

Figure 3.9 An example of the house of dreams, completed in an individual interview.

Widgit Symbols © Widgit Software Ltd 2002-2024 www.widgit.com

Having a visual symbol of each topic may be helpful. The pupil should remove each topic as it is 'finished'. This gives structure and familiarity to the pupils and may help to alleviate anxiety which may be induced by the unfamiliar situation (Figure 3.10).

Before you start the interview, explain the ground rules and reassure the pupil. It may be helpful to sit next to the pupil during the interview or sit on the floor together. Explain why you are interviewing or meeting with them. Remind them that they don't need to answer all the questions and that they can take a break or stop whenever they want to. Explain that you would like to collect everyone's answers together so that you can try to work out what we need to change about the school as this may help the pupils. Explain that you will show their answers to them and that they can change their answers later if they wish to. If your pupils are aware of their diagnosis, you may find it helpful to introduce the term, autism-affirming school.

Figure 3.10 Visual symbols of the topics which may be raised by your pupils.

Widgit Symbols © Widgit Software Ltd 2002–2024 www.widgit.com

The rationale for using a semi-structured interview format

A semi-structured interview format (Appendix 1) is helpful in the group and individual interviews as the structure is helpful in reassuring and guiding the pupils, while the fluid nature allows for clarification of any misunderstandings which may arise from the rigid thinking which may be typical of some of our pupils. This semi-structured format should enable you, as the interviewer, to keep the interview flexible, pose follow-up and clarifying questions and become involved in longer conversations with the pupils on topics that are of particular interest to them.

An open, unstructured approach to interviewing may be less helpful to our pupils who often benefit from working within a pre-determined structure with a clear finish point (Adderley et al., 2015). Conversely, a more rigid format would not allow for you to follow the pupils' thoughts and interests.

The interview is more likely to be successful if it takes place in a context which is well known and familiar to the pupils so try to conduct the interviews in a location which is familiar to, and regularly accessed by the pupils (Drever, 2003). Pre-warn the pupil about the interview, tell them when and where the interview will take place and include it in their individual timetable, if they have one. This familiarity and premeditated preparation is important for pupils, who may have difficulties managing unexpected events, and will hopefully help to alleviate the anxiety which unexpected change can bring.

A trusted and familiar adult should conduct the interviews. An additional adult in the interview could be asked to indicate if they notice any behaviour which may indicate that the pupil is feeling any anxiety, discomfort or distress.

I made an audio recording of the interviews and transcribed the interview in full, on the day of recording, to ensure accuracy, but this transcription is not necessary.

As part of the approach, wherever possible, try to go back to the pupils after the interviews to authenticate their narrative, sense-check their responses and make any adjustments requested by the pupil.

Be aware that any data collected should be stored according to General Data Protection Regulation guidelines and individual school practice and policy.

Both the group and individual interviews follow the same format, as many of the pupils find familiarity and predictability helpful. Therefore, the interview script is simple and repetitive. This does not mean that you cannot deviate from the script – follow the pupil's lead – but always return to the familiar three questions. The same three questions are repeated for each topic in turn (Appendix 1).

Adaptations and adjustments

The three houses approach, with simple adjustments to accommodate individual characteristics, should enable you to gather the views of pupils in your school and, therefore, help you to generate an understanding of what you need to do to create an autism-affirming school, from your pupils' perspective.

Some of the adaptations which may be useful include:

- Preparation. Ensure a tablet or phone is charged so you can record the interview. Have plenty of plain paper, A3 or A4, pencils and visual symbols to hand if these are being used. Ensure a quiet space is available – in many schools, this may be the biggest challenge!

- Pre-warning of the interview. Give advance warning to the pupil if this is helpful. Meet with the pupil earlier on the day of the interview to explain what is going to happen in the interview. If the pupil has an individual visual timetable, add the interview to their schedule.
- Simplified language. Use the simple script (Appendix 1) in the interview. Adapt the language to meet the ability, age and maturity of your pupils.
- Reduced language. For some pupils, strip back the language and focus on using visuals of the topics. The pupils can place these in the three houses visual.
- Familiar vocabulary. Ensure that the pupils are familiar with the terms being used.
- Be repetitive. Follow the script which asks the same questions repeatedly for each of the topics.
- Familiarity of room. Pupils will feel more comfortable in the interview if they are in a space which is familiar to them. For some pupils, it is important that they are not visible to their friends and peers.
- Familiarity of interviewer. Pupils are more likely to respond honestly if the adult conducting the interview is known to them. An adult who typically offers support but is not the class teacher may be the best person to conduct the interview. Alternatively, the SENCO may be a trusted and familiar adult.
- Preferred and non-preferred subjects. Ask your pupil to name their least favourite time of the week. This is a good time of the week to conduct the interview as they may be more willing to stay with you for the duration of the lesson, assembly and so on. Never interview a pupil during their preferred time of the week. The pupil will be focused on returning to their preferred activity as quickly as possible and may offer inaccurate responses to finish the interview as quickly as possible. I've learnt this the hard way!
- A visual to mark time. It may be helpful for the pupil to be made aware of how many questions they are going to be asked, topics they are going to discuss or minutes they are going to be in the interview.
- Finish by break/lunch time. There are pupils who do not enjoy breaktime and lunchtime, while for other pupils this is a necessary time for them to process the day, have time alone or run around with friends. Know the pupil's preference and act accordingly.
- Offer to scribe. Always offer a pencil or pen to the pupil. They may request that you start to scribe for them but, as they feel more comfortable, they may choose to take over or add to what you have written. If an adult is scribing for the pupil, it is important to write down exactly what the pupil says so it is an accurate account of the pupil's perspective and not an adult's interpretation. Some pupils may prefer to scribe for themselves as writing down their thoughts may be easier than giving a verbal response. Other pupils may not be able to write down their thoughts.
- Give additional processing time. It is important to know the length of time that it takes for the pupil to process and respond to the auditory information. For some pupils this may be several seconds.
- Allow time to talk briefly about the pupil's own interests before redirecting their attention. It may be helpful to have a visual timer for this.

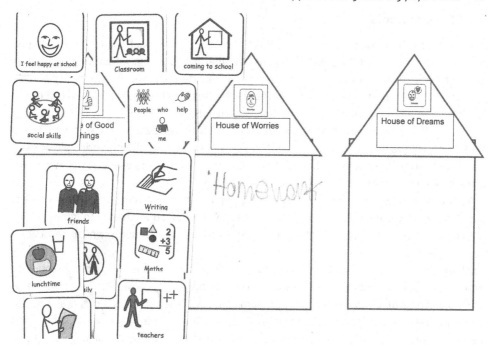

Figure 3.11 The three houses completed by a pupil who communicated his perspectives on school by sorting the symbols.

Widgit Symbols © Widgit Software Ltd 2002–2024 www.widgit.com

The three houses approach works well and may be adapted effectively to enable pupils with multiple means of communication to share their views. As I have highlighted, it is helpful to use visual symbols to represent each of the topics. This may enable some of your pupils, including those experiencing situational mutism, to share their views by placing the symbols in the appropriate houses (Figure 3.11).

The three jars

Having used the three houses approach with many pupils over several years, one of my colleagues, Joanna, has made her own adaptations to the approach. She found that some of the younger pupils found the three houses too abstract. As we have worry jars in each classroom, she had the idea of using three jars rather than three houses. She sometimes draws three jars in the same way that we draw the three houses. We have also used glass jars. In this case, the adult could write the responses on pieces of paper and place them in the appropriate jar. Although this is engaging, particularly for younger children, it is disadvantageous in that the pupil is not able to see so readily the summary of their responses. Nevertheless, be aware of any pupils who may benefit from this simple adaptation.

The three schools

As I explain below, visuals of houses are used because the approach stems from child protection where children are supported to consider what is happening within their home environment. I am yet to interview a pupil who has questioned why we use the house visuals. However, it may be pertinent to question whether houses are the most suitable visual tool to use. It may be more meaningful to use schools as visuals.

A word of caution, however: we would not want pupils to associate school with worries and think that they are in a school of worries. Houses, jars or schools, it is the principle of using visuals to support the pupils in sharing their views on what is going well, not going well and what we need to change that is important (Figure 3.12).

The three houses approach highlights that the pupils have perspectives in common and can identify what is important to them as well as what we need to change to improve their experience of school. This highlights the adaptations and adjustments which we need to make to our practice.

All of the pupils interviewed enjoyed and were engaged with the three houses approach during the group and individual interviews. During the group interviews, the pupils were able to initiate topics which were important to them, discuss these topics as a group and decide which house each topic should be placed in. They recognised that some topics sat in more than one house and did not always agree on which house the topic should be placed in. However, there was usually an overall consensus.

Using the three houses approach in the individual interviews (following the group interviews) facilitated further discussion on each topic and enabled the pupils to share their own perspectives of the school. The fluid nature of the semi-structured interview format meant

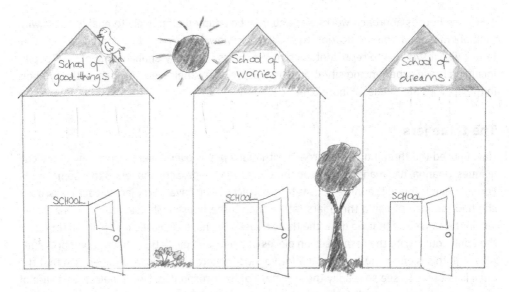

Figure 3.12 Author's drawing of the three schools.

Adapted from the three houses, Turnell, A. and Edwards, S. 1999; Weld, D. (2008).

that new topics could emerge during the individual interviews. The repetitive nature of the interview, discussing each topic in relation to the three houses, is helpful as familiarity and routine usually bring reassurance to the pupils.

The approach, with simple adjustments to accommodate individual characteristics (preparation, pre-warning, simplified language, familiar vocabulary, familiarity of room and interviewer), enables the meaningful participation of our pupils. Some pupils may require additional processing time to respond to the questions and pupils may need time to talk briefly about a subject of their own choosing before their attention is redirected to the task. You may need to scribe for some pupils. Others may find it helpful to scribe for themselves. This was helpful for one pupil who was not able to verbalise her views until her anxiety subsided. She was, however, willing to write down her thoughts.

Ethical considerations

Voluntary, informed consent should be sought from all stakeholders (school, parent and pupil) and standard ethical considerations should be specified and applied to your work with the pupils (British Educational Research Association, 2018; British Psychological Society, 2021; British Sociological Association, 2017). Specific adjustments may need to be in place to ensure the wellbeing of all pupils. Be prepared to stop or pause the interview at any time if you notice any behaviour which indicates feelings of anxiety, discomfort or distress.

In addition, the following ethical considerations are recommended by Turnell and Murphy (2014) when using the three houses approach:

- Inform the parents or carers before you engage with the child and explain the three houses approach to them. In engaging with children in a principle of the SEND Code of Practice (2015), it may not be necessary to gain permission as working collaboratively with children and their families should be an established way of working. However, your school may deem this to be necessary.
- Explain the three houses approach to the pupil. Using one sheet of paper per house often works well.
- Use words and drawings as appropriate to the pupil and anything else that may be useful to engage them in the process.
- Always start with the house of good things.
- After the interview, gain permission from the pupil to share their views [and tell them who you are going to share with].
- Present the three houses just as the child said, wrote or drew it. [This is to ensure that their views, thoughts and feelings are not conceptualised through an adult.]

A brief history of the three houses approach to gathering pupil voice

When I started gathering the voice of our pupils, I was aware that another group of children and young people also felt that they were not involved in decisions which affected them, and that their voice was not being heard. This group was children and young people caught up in the child protection system (Turnell and Edwards, 1999).

Turnell and Edwards (2014) recognise that practitioners often fail to involve children in discussions which affect them because they are rarely provided with straightforward tools and practical guidance to support them in gathering the child's voice. A number of tools, approaches and processes have since been designed to engage children and young people involved in child protection services. These include the specifically devised, participatory approach, the three houses, which is used to encourage discussion and collaboration around topics which are important to the children themselves.

It is the three houses approach I adapted and used to gather the voice of our pupils.

Reflections

Do you have a tool which you can use to gather the views, thoughts and feelings of your pupils?

Do you think that the three houses approach may be helpful in gathering pupil voice in your school?

What adaptations to the approach would you need to make to accommodate the needs of your pupils?

Do you think that your pupils would raise similar topics to those highlighted in this chapter?

Are you surprised by any of the themes which emerged?

How do you think these would align with the findings in your school?

Summary

As discussed in previous chapters, it is incumbent on us, as teachers, to find the means for our autistic pupils to express their perspectives of school in ways that are appropriate to their strengths, needs, age and maturity. This means finding ways to gather their views, thoughts and feelings and supporting them to communicate these perspectives so that they can take an active role in their lives and be involved in decisions that affect them, in this instance creating autism-affirming schools. Listening to their views, thoughts and feelings can help us to generate an understanding of how our pupils are experiencing school so that we can make the necessary adaptations and adjustments to our schools to improve their experience.

It is important that we give our pupils the opportunity to initiate and share their views on topics, things about the school, that are important to them. I agree with many researchers, working in the field of academic research, who highlight that we need to listen to autistic pupil voice more readily as there may be a lack of understanding of how to meet the needs of our autistic pupils. Finding the means for autistic pupils to share their views is necessary if we are to understand how our pupils are experiencing school and make the necessary changes to ensure that they have a positive experience of school.

As discussed previously, autistic individuals are increasingly sharing their own experiences of school in auto-biographical accounts. While these accounts are helpful in generating an understanding of how autistic children and young people are experiencing the non-autistic world, they may not be specifically insightful into their experience of primary school or highlight what we need to change in school to meet their needs. Furthermore, many of these accounts are historic reflections on experiences of school, some from many years previously.

My hope is that the three houses approach could be used more widely to support primary-aged autistic pupils in voicing their experience of school and enable them to communicate their own meaning of their experience.

The focus throughout this book is on engaging with an approach, the three houses, which recognises that every child is the unique. No two autistic children are the same and each school is different. The key is to ensure the value of this approach by listening to the voice of each autistic pupil and working collaboratively with them to understand what an autism-affirming school should be like from their perspective. The point is to use the three houses as an effective means of gathering pupil voice that is meaningful to both the pupils and the setting.

In this chapter, I have outlined:

How to use the three houses approach to identify topics which autistic pupils themselves identify as important to them.

The topics (things about the school) which autistic pupils identify as being important.

How to use the three houses approach to gather pupil voice in semi-structured group and individual interviews.

How to identify themes and sub-themes which may help us to generate a deeper understanding of how our pupils are experiencing school.

Ways in which the approach can be adjusted and adapted to meet each pupil's individual needs.

References

Adderley, R., Hope, M., Hughes, G., Jones, L., Messiou, K. and Shaw, P. (2015). Exploring inclusive practices in primary schools: Focusing on children's voices. *European Journal of Special Needs Education*, 30(1), 106–121.

Braun, V. and Clarke, V. (2006). Using thematic analysis in psychology. *Qualitative Research in Psychology*, 3(2), 77–101.

British Educational Research Association. (2018). *Ethical Guidelines for Educational Research* (4th ed.). British Educational Research Association.

British Psychological Society. (2021). *Code of Ethics and Conduct*. The British Psychological Society. https://explore.bps.org.uk/binary/bps.orks/bf9d9fead1dfec7c/3acfadeebe810a324dde720ea7b34b6e87a80cad1de54

British Sociological Association. (2017). *Statement of Ethical Practice*. British Sociological Association Publications.

Department of Education & Department for Health and Social Care. (2015). SEND Code of Practice: 0 to 25 years. Department of Education. https://assets.publishing.service.gov.uk/government/uploads/system/uploads/attachment_data/file/729208/SEN_2018_Text.pdf

Drever, E. (2003). *Using Semi-structured Interviews in Small-scale Research: A Teacher's Guide*. The SCRE Centre.

Goodall, C. (2018a). 'I felt closed in and like I couldn't breathe': A qualitative study exploring the mainstream educational experiences of autistic young people. *Autism and Developmental Language Impairments*, 3, 1–16.

Goodall, C. (2018b). Inclusion is a feeling, not a place: A qualitative study exploring autistic young people's conceptualisations of inclusion. *International Journal of Inclusive Education*. DOI:10.1080/13603116.2018.1523475

Goodall, C. (2020). *Understanding the Voices and Educational Experiences of Autistic Young People: From Research to Practice*. Routledge.

Harrington, C., Foster, M., Rodger, S. and Ashburner, J. (2014). Engaging young people with autism spectrum disorder in research interviews. *British Journal of Learning Disabilities, 42*(2),153–161.

Horgan, F., Kenny, N. and Flynn, P. (2023). A systematic review of the experiences of autistic young people enrolled in mainstream second-level (post-primary) schools. *Autism, 27*(2), 526–538. https://doi.org/10.1177/13623613221105089

Humphrey, N. and Lewis, S. (2008). Make me normal: The views and experiences of pupils on the autistic spectrum in mainstream secondary schools. *Autism, 12*(1), 23–46.

Keats, D. (2000). *Interviewing: A Practical Guide for Students and Professionals*. Open University Press.

Kvale, S. (2007). *Doing Interviews*. Sage Publications Ltd.

Saggers, B., Hwang, Y. and Mercer, L. (2011). Your voice counts: Listening to the voice of high school students with autism spectrum disorder. *Australasian Journal of Special Education, 35*(2), 173–190. www.cambridge.org/core/terms

Turnell, A. and Edwards, S. (1999). *Signs of Safety: A Safety and Solution-oriented Approach to Child Protection Casework*. W.W. Norton.

Turnell, A. (2004). Relationship-grounded, safety-organised child protection practice: dreamtime or real-time option for child welfare? *Protecting Children, 19*(2), 14–25.

Turnell, A. and Murphy, T. (2014). Comprehensive briefing paper signs of safety signs safety resolutions consultancy, East Perth, WA Australia. www.safeguardingsolihull.org.uk/lscp/wp-content/uploads/sites/3/2021/09/Signs-of-Safety-Briefing-Paper-v3-1-1.pdf

Weld, N. (2008). The three houses tool: Building safety and positive change. In Calder, M. (Ed.). *Contemporary Risk Assessment in Safeguarding Children*. Russell House Publishing.

Chapter four

What the pupils said

Understand me, I may surprise you

Chapter outline

The chapter opens with a discussion on the implications for practice, and consideration of the adaptations and adjustments which were requested by the pupils themselves. I discuss pupils' perspectives on teachers' understanding of autism and the high levels of anxiety which our pupils are working hard to hide; the positive characteristics of a 'good teacher' from the pupils' perspective; relationships with friends and peers; developing a whole-school, inclusive culture with diversity being the norm; autistic identity and pupil self-advocacy.

I explain how teachers can use pupil voice to support them in developing their understanding of how their pupils may be feeling misunderstood. I include a range of strategies which use the pupils' perspective to support teachers in generating a greater understanding of autism in general and of their autistic pupils specifically. These include communication analysis models, pupil passports, the three houses framework and the PATH approach to pupil-centred target and outcome setting.

The chapter closes with pupils' perspectives on the theme. I include quotes from many pupils from different schools, so that their views, thoughts and feelings are recorded accurately and not translated through an adult. Their narrative serves as a powerful testimony to how they often experience a lack of understanding of themselves as autistic pupils and explains why the implication of the Teachers' Toolbox may be helpful in creating autism-affirming schools.

Themes and sub-themes

As I highlighted at the end of the previous chapter, three key themes emerged which we should listen to and act upon if we are to create autism-affirming schools from our pupils' perspective.

Understand me - I may surprise you.
Help me to understand - understand myself and understand others.
Hide support for me - or I won't use it.

DOI: 10.4324/9781003396499-4

Each of the three overarching themes is broken down to a number of sub-themes 'underneath' the central theme. The subthemes focus on different elements of the overarching theme. Each of the sub-themes is notable in that it was mentioned by multiple pupils on several different occasions in a number of different schools.

The theme 'Understand me – I may surprise you has three sub-themes':

Teachers – pupils requested that we, their teachers, understand them as autistic pupils.

> Well by the way they're acting. I can just tell. Vibrations are going in my head to say that they [teachers] need to learn more.

Hidden anxiety – pupils requested that we, their teachers, understand the high level of anxiety which they are working hard to hide.

> Worrying can suck the joy out of me.

Friends/peers – pupils requested that their friends and peers understand them and are supported to learn more about autism.

> It's very important that they know [that I am autistic] because some people may see people acting differently and thinking it's just weird, but it isn't.

The themes 'Help me to understand – understand myself and understand others' and 'Hide Support for me – or I won't use it' will be considered in subsequent chapters.

In this chapter, I discuss and reflect on the theme: 'Understand me – I may surprise you'.

Understand me

Teachers – pupils requested that teachers understand them as autistic pupils

Teachers' understanding of autism impacts positively and negatively on the pupils' experience of school. The pupils recognise that we, their teachers, have the biggest single impact on their time at school, and pupils share negative experiences of some teachers. They feel very strongly that many teachers and other members of staff do not know enough about autism, and that 'everyone needs to learn more'. Teachers who understand autism generally, and the strengths and needs of their pupils specifically, are requested by pupils.

When autistic children and young people were questioned, as part of the 2023 National Autistic Society School Report, its research found that **only 26 per cent of autistic pupils feel happy at school** (National Autistic Society, 2023). Critically, the pupils highlight a general lack of understanding of autism in schools. Seven in ten of autistic pupils said that school would be better if more teachers understood autism and **the biggest thing that would make school better is having a teacher who understands autism.**

These views reflect the findings of the All-Party Parliamentary Group on Autism (2017) which found that six in ten pupils reported that the main thing they would change about school would be having a teacher who understands autism. Eleven of the 12 pupils in Goodall's (2020) study spoke of teachers who did not understand them or their autism.

The hope that teachers may improve their understanding of autism was universally held by pupils

However, pupils are also able to identify teachers they feel had a good understanding of autism. Pupils are able to list the characteristics of a 'good teacher' from their perspective. There is a consensus on the characteristics, knowledge and skills which define a 'good teacher', primarily one who demonstrates an understanding of their autistic pupils.

Developing a greater understanding of autism among teachers, and other members of staff working in schools, is critical if we are to improve pupils' experience of school and begin to alleviate their feelings of worry, stress and anxiety. Using the pupils as a valuable resource to develop a fuller understanding of their experiences of school could be an important step in developing our knowledge. Having teachers who understand autism is critical if we are to create autism-affirming schools.

The characteristics of a 'good teacher'

Pupils are able to identify the positive teacher characteristics which they recognise as being important in a 'good' teacher. They identify teachers who have an insightful understanding of autism, are able to relate to them as autistic pupils and understand their strengths and difficulties. Pupils report that understanding their needs is an important teacher characteristic and feel that this understanding could be achieved by listening to their perspectives.

The pupils want teachers to treat everyone fairly and this needs to be evident to them. Most pupils request a fair and consistent approach. Pupils also request flexibility to support their specific needs.

The pupils want the teachers to create a calm and structured learning environment with few distractions and reduced sensory input. They report that they find it anxiety-provoking if teachers raise their voice.

Pupils request that they need support and want teachers to deliver it in a subtle and skilful way.

Making learning engaging, motivating, fun and enjoyable helps the pupils with focus and attention, especially in the subjects which they do not enjoy or are not particularly good at; this tends to be subjects which involve writing. This approach could also support the pupils with their acquisition and retention of knowledge and skills. A good teacher is also kind.

The consensus of what pupils identify a good teacher should be like may warrant further consideration and it may be interesting to complete this exercise in your own school.

I wonder if the characteristics would be different if non-autistic pupils were asked to describe a 'good teacher'?

It may also be helpful to self-assess against this check list, as well as asking a colleague to complete the assessment.

Personal attributes were particularly important to the pupils. In addition, the pupils recognise a number of key skills: These are identified as follows (Table 4.1):

Table 4.1 'A good teacher' checklist

Personal attributes and skills	Self-assessed	Colleague-assessed
Insightful understanding of autism		
Understands and supports individual strengths and difficulties		
Listens to the pupil and is responsive to what they say		
Kind and caring		
Speaks with a calm and measured voice		
Flexible to support specific needs		
Makes learning fun, engaging and motivating		
Treats all pupils fairly and this is evident		
Firm and consistent approach		
Creates a predictable, structured and calm learning environment		
Understands support needed and offers support in a subtle and skilful manner		

Understand me

Pupils request that we, their teachers, understand the high level of anxiety which they are working hard to hide

Feelings of anxiety, often due to feeling misunderstood, are reported by many pupils. The pupils describe how their anxiety is heightened in the classroom as the pressure of work (amount and difficulty) increases. For some pupils, the sensory experience of the classroom, the noise, temperature and the confusion of the teacher's message add to feelings of stress.

The compulsion to hide their anxiety from us, friends and peers leads to further feelings of distress and they request that we understand the need for specific adaptations and adjustments, subtly and skillfully delivered. The pupils feel that a greater understanding on the part of their teachers may lead to a reduction in their anxiety which they feel compelled to hide. The pupils are very firm in their belief that teachers do not always understand the anxiety that they are experiencing. The pupils may appear to be coping in the classroom, and around the school, but this is often not the case. There is also a consensus that a lack of understanding on our part is leading to heightened levels of pupil anxiety which are unnecessary and avoidable.

Pupils become so adept in hiding or masking their autism, and presenting a 'non-autistic' self, that their teachers believe that they are coping, when they are not (National Autistic Society). While this may be sub-conscious for younger children, this did not appear to be a passive response for many pupils; they are working hard to keep up the pretence that they are able to cope with the social, sensory and academic demands of the classroom and the school. The pupils are anxious about not being able to cope, and worried that their inability to cope may be discovered. If we fail to understand that autism comes with heightened levels of anxiety and that our pupils may be working hard to hide this anxiety, the long-term impact on our pupils may be detrimental, leading to poor mental health outcomes as highlighted previously.

Although **70 per cent of autistic pupils said that teachers do not understand enough about autism** and 54 per cent said that having teachers who don't understand them is the worst thing about school, when the National Autistic Society surveyed teachers, it found that

87 per cent felt confident in supporting autistic pupils (National Autistic Society, 2023). This finding may demonstrate we are not aware of the gaps in our understanding of our pupils and what they need.

There is clearly a disconnect between teachers' confidence in supporting pupils and how well supported pupils feel. This may be due to many of us not having insightful and meaningful autism training. As autism is a spectrum condition, every child or young person may present differently. Many autistic pupils will hide and mask difficulties and present their non-autistic selves. We need support and effective training to help us to understand the adjustments which we can make to support our autistic pupils.

An enhanced understanding of the pupils' perspective, and of autism generally, may challenge our assumptions about how our pupils are coping in the classroom. Teachers often assume that social and cognitive skills are aligned and, therefore, some of our pupils do not need additional support or adjustments in school. A better understanding of autism generally, and the needs of the individual specifically, would go some way to preventing autistic children becoming unnecessarily overwhelmed and distressed.

By listening to our pupils and generating an understanding of them, we may begin to understand the cause of their anxiety. Pupils told us that their teachers' lack of understanding, the demands of the curriculum (pace and difficulty), the social and environmental demands of the classroom, break- and lunchtimes, homework and the transition to and from school all contributed to their anxiety. Pupils' anxiety generally heightens as each of these demands increases.

The National Autistic Society (2023) suggests that to develop an understanding of autism in general and their autistic pupils specifically, teachers need substantive training which is co-produced by autistic children and young people. The training should cover, in detail, how autistic pupils can mask and hide their difficulties and often experience very high levels of stress and anxiety.

What is masking?

Masking may also be referred to as 'camouflaging', 'social camouflaging', using 'compensatory strategies' or 'passing' (Belcher, 2022). Autistic people describe how they feel compelled to put on a mask to hide or cover up their autistic selves. Masking could be described as endeavouring to act in ways (that usually come intuitively to non-autistic people), in order to meet social expectations and blend into the non-autistic world.

Masking can happen in any situation but it is more likely to happen in situations where autistic people believe that they are not understood. Research suggests that autistic people learn how to mask by observing, analysing and mirroring the behaviours of others. This may be in real life or characters in television, films, books or games. They may use these copied, non-autistic behaviours such as facial expressions, eye contact, speech, scripts and tone of voice while suppressing helpful behaviours, which may be viewed as odd or unusual by non-autistic people.

Our autistic pupils may use masking, consciously or unconsciously, as a strategy to appear 'less autistic' to cope (and be accepted) in the non-autistic world. Masking is exhaustingly effortful and can lead to autistic shutdown, burnout and poor mental health in the long term.

We can support our pupils by ensuring that the adaptations and adjustments which they request are in place. We should be creating schools which embrace, celebrate and promote autism and neurodiversity so pupils feel more able to show their autistic selves during the school day without judgement or comment from others.

Understand me

Pupils requested that their friends and peers understand about autism

When considering friends and peers, the narrative is more mixed. There is agreement that generating a greater understanding of autism among friends and peers is necessary, and older pupils feel that it is important that their peers understand more about autism so that their (autistic) behaviours are not viewed as 'weird'.

In the 2023 National Autistic Society survey, just **8 per cent of autistic students felt that their friends and peers understood enough about autism**. This figure highlights that there is a general lack of understanding about autism in schools and autistic pupils are pay-ing a price for this. Interactions with friends and peers are an important element of the school experience and it is important that autistic pupils feel understood by their friends and peers. Without this understanding, pupils can feel compelled to hide or mask their difficulties, unable to present their autistic selves.

> I would think, if we actually got educated on what autism and other neurodiver-
> gence are like, I think people would actually know what it was or what it was like to
> see the world differently ... They'd know how to not just look out for someone but
> also how to support someone.
> (Autistic student, National Autistic Society school report, 2023)

Most pupils understand that friends are a supportive factor, even if they do not have a best friend or sometimes prefer spending some time alone. However, it is clear that some pupils are also finding friendships difficult to navigate and do not always understand who their friends are or the characteristics of a positive friendship.

Generally, secondary school pupils report more negative feelings towards friendships and their peers. They commonly report feelings of isolation although many do have a friend or friendship group, often sustained through a shared interest.

In order to support friendships and peer relationships, the following may be helpful.

- Offer clubs during the school day for pupils who have interests in common and which may support autistic pupils. Clubs such as chess, Lego, gaming, programming, art and cookery may be preferred. Be mindful of introducing clubs which may be stereotypical. Ask your pupils what they would like to do.
- Enable pupils to build relationships with other pupils who have interests in common, for example some of our pupils are interested in Pokémon, football, gaming, Harry Potter, animals, maps. Notice that these interests may change over time.
- Create calm, quite spaces where pupils can meet with other pupils or spend time alone.
- Introduce a lunchtime club where turn-taking games are supported by an adult.
- Enable pupils to act as buddies to younger children, with pupils working in pairs.

Developing an inclusive culture with diversity being the norm: an understanding from 'both sides'

We need to develop an inclusive culture with diversity being the norm if we are to create autism-affirming schools, improve the experience of school for our autistic pupils and enable them to be their wonderful autistic selves.

Overwhelmingly, pupils request a greater understanding of autism, from every member of staff and from their friends and peers. They request that everyone, including them, should be enabled to understand more.

If pupils feel supported and understood within the school, it may help them to positively embrace their autism, help them to improve self-esteem and begin to feel more positively about any feelings of difference which they may be holding onto. Viewing difference and diversity positively may help to alleviate the feelings of negativity, self-doubt and vulnerability that can arise from feeling the need to hide and mask their autism and show a non-autistic self. It is, after all, normal to be different.

Autism should be considered positively as a culture; a way of communicating and understanding the world which may be shared with other autistic pupils.

Pupils request a positive culture of diversity in school where they are supported to develop an understanding of the non-autistic world, and teachers, friends and peers are supported to increase their understanding of the autistic world. Pupils are keen to learn about the non-autistic world but feel that their desire to understand more was not usually reciprocated by non-autistic individuals. In her book *The Girl with the Curly Hair*, Rowe (2013) suggests that we need to make a bridge between the autistic and non-autistic communities and in *Pretending to Be Normal*, Willey (1999) advocates adjustments on both sides: from autistic and non-autistic individuals alike. The need for adaptations and adjustments on both sides has obvious implications for practice.

As self-advocacy is growing within the autistic community, there is an increasing narrative, which was initially put forward by Milton (2012), that non-autistic individuals tend to lack insight into, and understanding of, the autistic world. Pupils agree whole-heartedly with Milton and state that many of their teachers, friends and peers lack an understanding of autism and them as autistic pupils with many strengths.

Milton recognises that it may be difficult for a non-autistic person to understand how an autistic person is perceiving and making sense of the world. However, he argues that too much emphasis is placed on the autistic person understanding the non-autistic world and very little value is placed on understanding the autistic world.

Where is the social learning of the autistic world?

Milton describes this as the 'double-empathy problem' (Milton, 2012, p. 883) and argues that it is autistic people who have gained a greater insight into the non-autistic world which raises the question about a lack of social motivation from non-autistic individuals. Viewed in this way, adaptations and adjustments are helpful from 'both sides' and non-autistic individuals should alter their behaviour and practice accordingly. In other words, we should not be expecting autistic pupils to make all the running but we should be meeting somewhere in the middle, by making the changes to our practice which the pupils themselves request.

Brook (in Wood, 2019. p. 70) advocates that:

> Autistic kids need to be supported as autistic kids, recognising that everyone's normal is different. All aspects of school, seem to be only recognised as significant if we fit into some weird standardised 'normal'. I think this is an issue for many kids, not just autistic ones.

If our autistic pupils are not thriving in our schools, we should not consider this as a deficit held within the autistic pupil but should think about the adaptations and adjustments which we need to make 'from our side' to enable them to have a positive and enjoyable school experience.

Understand me: autistic identity within an inclusive culture of diversity

As I have highlighted throughout the book, first and foremost, the pupils requested that the school in general, and their teachers specifically, generate a meaningful and insightful understanding of autism and make every effort to understand them as autistic pupils. This means understanding the need for pupils to be their autistic selves and engage in behaviours which support them, such as stimming, movement seeking or having access to a calm space. Stimming – or self-stimulatory behaviour – is engaging in repetitive body movements or noises. Stimming may help autistic children cope with and manage strong emotions like anxiety, anger, fear and excitement and may be a helpful self-soothing or self-regulatory strategy. Duffus (2023) suggests that we need to be actively promoting autistic pride and creating communities where autistic children and young people can understand their strengths and where they can expect others to make adjustments and adaptations so that their needs can be met. Duffus reports that having a positive understanding of individual autistic identity is an indicator of higher self-esteem and wellbeing in adulthood.

Many autistic advocates are beginning to discuss the term 'autistic identification' as positive and affirming, and prefer it to the term 'diagnosis', which may be problematic for some (Sandland, 2022). Identifying as an autistic person means that the child or young person can acknowledge the many parts that make up their identity, including, but not limited to, their autistic characteristics. Autistic children and young people may also find strength, comfort and support in being part of a community with things in common and a shared identity.

In my experience, children and young people are often not told that they are autistic and, therefore, receive no support in generating an understanding of what autism means to them. They are not supported in meeting other autistic children and young people if they choose to do so. Therefore, autistic children and young people are often left feeling different and alienated. The family of the autistic child or young person may be offered the opportunity to join a support group or signposted to parenting classes but what is the child or young person offered? It may be helpful for them to be made aware of autism at the start of their autistic journey of discovery so that they can generate an understanding of autism over time, with the support of professional and knowledgeable adults.

The child themselves may find a diagnosis beneficial in generating an understanding of themselves and giving them an improved sense of their own identity and a sense of belonging.

However, grouping all autistic children together is unhelpful. In the same way that we would not group all non-autistic children together and apply a 'one size fits all' model. Autistic children are unique and should be treated as such.

Belcher (2022) highlights that when non-autistic people know that someone is autistic, they seem to judge them less harshly. However, she recognises that any strategy to encourage autistic people to reveal their diagnosis must come hand in hand with a whole-school approach to generate an understanding of autism.

Developing a whole-school approach

The whole school community needs to generate an insightful and meaningful understanding of autism. Although it is vital that all staff working in schools have continued professional learning/development to generate an understanding of autism, this, in itself, is not enough.

The pupils can be supported as advocates and given the opportunity to communicate their lived experiences of the school to us, their teachers, and other members of staff. Their powerful testimonies serve as a highly effective catalyst to generating an understanding of the adjustments and adaptations that we need to make to meet our pupils 'half-way'.

A call to action

- Enable the pupils to act as advocates for themselves and others.
- Facilitate ways in which the pupils can voice their views, thoughts and feelings of the school.
- Enable the pupils to share their experience of school with teachers and other members of staff.
- Listen to our pupils and be prepared to change practice and make the adaptations and adjustments which the pupils themselves have requested.
- Engage all members of staff in continued professional learning/development to generate a meaningful understanding of autism.
- Celebrate and promote autism and neurodiversity within the school.
- Immerse the children by having books and resources in the classroom and throughout the school which represent and promote autistic and neurodiverse characters.
- Enable the pupils to share their stories with their friends and peers, when they are ready,
- Invite autistic and neurodiverse advocates into the school to share their stories and celebrate their successes.
- Talk about autism and neurodiversity using a strength-based approach, recognising the strengths and difficulties.
- Highlight well known autistic people and discuss the part they have played in our history.
- Invite older and past pupils back to school to share their stories.
- Promote, support and discuss autism and neurodiversity in assemblies, classroom discussions, family events, governor meetings, curriculum evenings, when promoting the school to new families and the wider community.
- Introduce the All About Me programme (Miller, 2018), discussed in the next chapter.

Teachers' Toolbox

How to support teachers in generating an understanding of their pupils

Teachers can use pupil voice to support them in developing their understanding of how their pupils may be feeling misunderstood. A greater understanding on the part of us, their teachers, may, in turn, lead to reduced levels of anxiety amongst our pupils.

I introduce and explain a range of strategies which use pupils' perspective to support us in generating a greater understanding of autism in general and of our autistic pupils specifically. These include two different communication analysis models; pupil passports; the three houses framework and the PATH approach to pupil-centred target and outcome setting. When worked through collaboratively with our pupils, the strategies may also serve to support them in increasing their understanding of themselves.

I am not suggesting that all these tools are implemented; I have included a selection of things which may be helpful. Different tools will be more helpful for some pupils in some settings.

I would always advocate a whole-school approach, where possible.
Adjusting practice across the school, in response to pupil voice, will benefit
autistic pupils but may also be beneficial to all pupils; it will certainly
not be detrimental to them.

The SPELL framework

SPELL is a framework which is advocated by the National Autistic Society and may be used as part of a whole-school approach to generate an understanding of our autistic pupils. The framework is aligned with what the pupils requested, namely that we generate a greater understanding of them as autistic pupils, that we help them to understand themselves and others and that we hide the necessary support for them.

The framework emphasises changes which we should make to meet the specific needs of our pupils, recognising that each pupil is unique. The SPELL framework can be used to support all pupils.

SPELL stands for:
Structure
Positive (approaches and expectations)
Empathy
Low arousal
Links

Structure

The pupils requested structure, predictability and routine. Structure makes the non-autistic world a more predictable, accessible and safer place. Structure can support autonomy, self-advocacy and independence by reducing dependence on adults. We can adapt our environments to communicate to our pupils what is going to happen and what is expected of them, thereby reducing anxiety. The SPELL framework advocates using visual communication as one way of creating structured environments. Visual communication was requested by the pupils and can be used as part of a whole-school approach.

Positive (approaches and expectations)

In line with a strengths-based approach, we should seek to develop self-confidence and self-esteem by building on individual strengths, interests and abilities. Expectations should be high but realistic and based on observation, so we generate an understanding of the things that our pupils are finding difficult. Understanding our pupils' skills, interests and strengths is important when considering how to support them with the things that they find difficult.

Empathy

We should try to develop a greater understanding of the autistic world in general and how our pupils are experiencing the non-autistic world specifically. Attempting to understand, respect and relate to our pupils must underpin our attempts to make the necessary adaptations and adjustments and reduce anxiety. The quality of the relationship between the pupils and their supporters (teachers) is key. Effective supporters are calm, predictable, good humoured, empathetic and analytical.

Low arousal

The environment should be calm and ordered to reduce anxiety and support focus and attention. There should be as few distractions as possible and we should pay attention to the sensory aspects of the school environment which our pupils find difficult. Many of our pupils need more time to process information, especially verbal information. Clear information should be given in a way which is best suited to them, with care taken not to overload or bombard them. Low arousal does not mean 'no arousal'. However, the sensory environment should be controlled in ways that are supportive to our pupils to reduce anxiety and support focus and attention.

Links

Forging links with our pupils and their families will reduce the risk of misunderstanding, confusion or the adoption of unhelpful approaches. We should create and maintain links to ensure that we are able to generate an insightful understanding of our pupils.

Adopting the SPELL framework could form part of a whole-school approach to supporting our pupils.

The STAR and ABC models – communication analysis models

The STAR and ABC models are used widely in the field of psychology as tools to understand what a pupil is communicating, both verbally and non-verbally through behaviour. Both models may be helpful in supporting us to generate an understanding of our pupils. The models

Table 4.2 The STAR approach – communication analysis chart

STAR Approach – communication analysis chart					
Day of week, date and time	Setting	Trigger	Action	Result	Observed by Comments
	Where was the pupil, and who else was present?	What happened before the incident? This may be before school or outside the classroom.	What behaviour is the pupil displaying? What is the pupil communicating verbally and non-verbally?	What is the result for the pupil? What is the function/need for the pupil? How did the adults respond? How did peers respond?	

can also be used to support the pupil in generating a greater understanding of themselves. This is, of course, dependant on the age, maturity and language ability of the pupil (Table 4.2).

The STAR approach is a helpful tool which can be used to develop an understanding of the pupil and what they are communicating. The basis of the approach is to understand that all communication (behaviour) can be seen as action with a purpose which is embarked upon in order to receive a specific response. The approach can be used to understand what the pupil is communicating, identify anxiety-provoking parts of the day, week or term, notice things that the pupil is finding particularly difficult and begin to understand patterns of behaviour over a period of time.

STAR stands for:
Setting
Trigger
Action
Result

Setting

This helps us to understand how the pupil is responding to the place and the people within the place. Consider the social and environmental demands as well as the relationships and interactions of the adults and the pupil. The pupil's response is dependent on the complex relationship between the pupil and the environment.

Trigger

These are the stimuli that trigger or 'set off' the specific episode. There are numerous triggers.

The pupil may have a need which they need to be met – they may be feeling hungry, hot, cold or unwell.

The pupil may be expressing something that they do not want to do or feel that they are unable to do. The pupil may have a fear that their teacher will discover that they are finding something difficult.

The pupil may be expressing something that they find particularly difficult, for example understanding the rules of an unfamiliar teacher, eating lunch in the lunch hall or an unexpected change to the timetable or routine.

Emotional overload – this is the 'last straw' after a series of events which the pupil has found difficult. The demands of the morning routine and transitioning into school may mean that the pupil is already in a heightened state and the trigger at this point may seem insignificant, for example an unexpected remark or a touch to the arm.

Action

What the pupil does to communicate to the adult. This may be a behaviour which should be considered as a non-verbal means of communication.

Results

This is what happens as a result of the action; a series of events that are usually in the control of the teacher. The response from the teacher should be seen as a communication to the child and can indicate the likelihood of the child repeating the cycle. Consider whether the child is getting what they want (need) as a result of their action. Is there a way that we can meet this need without the child's action? For example, if the child is throwing their food in the lunch hall and getting taken to a different environment as a result (and this is desirable for the child), could we find a calmer place for the child to eat their lunch? (Table 4.3)

ABC stands for:
Antecedent
Behaviour
Consequences

Table 4.3 The ABC Approach – communication analysis chart

ABC Approach – communication analysis chart			
Day of week, date and time Setting	*Antecedent*	*Behaviour (communication)*	*Consequences (function for child)*	*Observed by Comments*
	What happened before the incident? This may be before school or outside the classroom.	What behaviour is the pupil displaying? What is the pupil communicating verbally and non-verbally?	What is the result for the pupil? What is the function/need for the pupil? How did the adults respond? How did peers respond?	

The ABC approach is another tool for understanding what the pupil is communicating and what they are finding difficult and/or anxiety-provoking. In line with the STAR model, the ABC model can also be used to identify the triggers by monitoring external environmental stimuli (people, place, time, day, the classroom and school environment) which are impacting the pupil's internal stimuli (emotional and sensory regulation, the pupil's thoughts and feelings) and result in observable behaviour (communication).

Whichever approach is used, it may be appropriate that we, or another trusted adult, discuss the events with the pupil when the pupil is in a calm state. This may help us to understand what the pupil was feeling as events unfolded.

It may also be helpful to reflect on the consequences of the pupil's and teacher's behaviour, both short-term and long-term, intended and unintended. If appropriate to the age and maturity of the child, the models may be helpful in supporting the pupil to build an awareness of the parts of the day and week which they are finding the most difficult. This may help us to generate an understanding of the impact (negative and positive) that different parts of the day and week are having on the pupil. We can then make the necessary adaptations and adjustments to support the pupil.

Whichever model is used, it is incumbent on the adult to understand what the pupil is communicating in order to make adjustments which make things easier for the child.

A note of caution

Teachers generating a greater understanding of their pupils was requested by the pupils themselves. It will take a great deal of effort on our part to understand experiences which we do not share. We should, therefore, attempt to generate an understanding of the qualitatively different ways which our pupils use to interact, communicate and manage in the non-autistic world and that these may not coincide with our means of communication (Bogdashina, 2011).

The STAR and ABC approaches, highlighted above, may be used to understand more about our pupils and how they are experiencing school. The approaches may be used to recognise what our pupils are communicating, identify anxiety-provoking parts of the day, week or term and notice the things that they are finding particularly difficult. By reflecting on our observations of the pupils, we may begin to understand what they are communicating about their school experience through their behaviours.

Once we understand what the pupil is communicating, we can make changes to support the pupil by adjusting the sensory, social and environmental factors which we have control over. We are not attempting to change the pupil or diminish their experiences. The point is that we should respond to their behaviours by making adaptations and adjustments to support them and make the experience less anxiety-provoking. Once we have understood the situations which they are finding difficult and made changes, we may observe a pupil who is feeling more comfortable in the environment (Figure 4.1).

Placing the pupil at the centre may be helpful in generating an understanding of the adaptations and adjustments which we need to make. The DCCBA model does this.

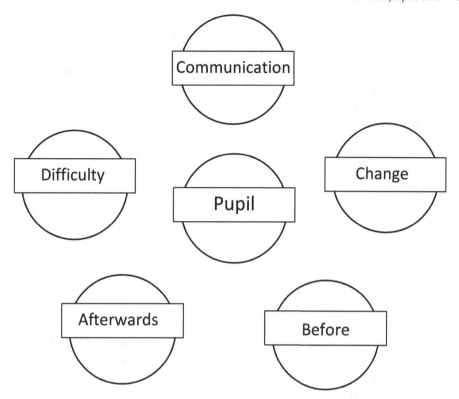

Figure 4.1 The DCCBA approach.

Source: Adapted by the author from the STAR and ABC communication analysis chart.

DCCBA stands for:

Difficulty – what is the pupil finding difficult/ anxiety provoking about the experience or situation? Consider the sensory, social and environmental experience.

Communication – how and what is the pupil communicating, verbally and non-verbally?

Change – what adaptations and adjustments do we need to make to make the experience or situation easier for the pupil?

Before – did preceding events exacerbate or alleviate the difficulty?

Afterwards – what happened afterwards for the pupil? Was the outcome positive or negative from the pupil's perspective? Is the outcome helpful for the pupil?

An example of the DCCBA approach

Difficulty – the pupil is not joining his peers in the weekly music lesson.

Communication – the pupil runs out of the music room or refuses to enter.

Change – change the sensory environment (offer ear defenders and offer a choice of seating position). Create more predictability and routine (prepare for change, visit the classroom and meet the teacher before the lesson to support familiarisation; use visual communication tools such as a visual timetable). Take a motivating activity (e.g. drawing) to the music lesson or use as a motivator on a now and next board. A 'now and next' board is a type of timetable. It gives the pupil structure by explaining what is happening now and what will be happening next, in a simple way using relatable visuals. The 'next' can be used to motivate the pupil to engage in the 'now'. Use backward chaining as a supportive strategy (the pupil joins the lesson for the final two minutes of the lesson. A visual timer is used to denote time. The time is built up gradually over a number of weeks). Backward chaining involves breaking the task down into small, manageable steps. Teach the child the final step of the task. You complete all the steps except the final one, which the child completes.

Before – introduce a period of calm before the music lesson.

Afterwards – the pupil is missing music and is engaging in a motivating activity (drawing) in a calm place. Consider whether this is a desirable outcome for the pupil.

Pupil support plan

It may be helpful to work collaboratively with a pupil to develop a support plan. The plan may help us to understand the situations which the pupil is finding particularly difficult. The aim of the support plan is individual to the pupil.

In this example, the aim is for the pupil to generate an understanding of when he needs to ask for help from an adult. We are targeting the end of the school year for this.

We will know that progress has been made when:

Adults understand the communication that they are seeing and what this may mean for the pupil.

Adults reflect on the situation for the pupil and understand how they, as adults, are impacting on this.

Adults reflect on how the pupil's needs can be met and what adaptations and adjustments they need to be made to support the pupil.

The pupil is able to acknowledge when they need to ask an adult for help.

The pupil to be able to reflect on the situation and understand how they and others are impacting on it.

The pupil is able to take action to help themselves (Table 4.4).

Table 4.4 An example of a pupil support plan

What we may observe	How we can help
What the pupil says and does that gives us clues that the pupil is feeling calm and relaxed/ready to engage/learn/play.	The things adults can do or say to help the pupil to feel calm and relaxed in the situation. Note that this may be an unfamiliar feeling for some of our pupils when they are in school. Using the language of feeling ok may be more helpful.
Pupil will engage, may smile and laugh. Sit on chair, at table, on carpet space or in calm corner. Chat appropriately with you. Body language will be relaxed and open.	Allow processing time – of information and instructions. Think ahead to anticipate what might be difficult for the pupil. Monitor stress levels/anxiety and scale back demands accordingly.

(Continued)

Table 4.4 (Continued)

Talk and interact with those around him. Answer questions. Attend to task, learning or play for an agreed duration. Respond appropriately to adults and peers. Follow instructions.	Make sure there is space in the classroom/school where pupil can go to feel calm. Prepare the pupil for what is going to happen, as this gives a sense of being in control, as well as allowing processing time. Give the pupil specific verbal feedback that reinforces the positive choices being made. Use indirect language e.g. I wonder if you can ... Let's see if we can ... Let's see if we can beat the clock ... Maybe we could investigate ... Let's watch first ... Use visual timetable and now/next board. Praise and affirm – be specific.
What we may observe What pupil says or does that gives us clues that he is feeling 'fizzy' or 'rumbling'.	**How we can help** The things adults can do to stop a situation escalating so pupil can re-engage in learning/play as soon as possible.
Take self to the toilet. Unable to follow instructions. Move around the classroom. Do what he is asked not to do. Throw objects. Have less regard for others. Shout/shout out. Seek attention for these behaviours.	Give time (to process information). Give time to self/co-regulate. Know what is important to pupil, e.g. going to lunch with friends. Remove or reduce language. Use visuals to communicate. Give choice of two options. Use humour and distraction. Suggest moving to calm space. Stay calm. We must regulate ourselves first, so that we can then help the pupil to regulate his anxiety. Model calm – reflect what we want to see. Be aware of any triggers. Do not introduce a sanction at this stage that is going to lead to further dysregulation.
What we may observe What pupil says or does that gives us clues that he is in distress.	**What we can do to help** The things we can do or say to quickly manage the situation and to prevent further escalation.
May attempt to run out of the room/building. Scream. Throw objects. Shout. Run around. Engage in unsafe behaviours. Unable to follow instructions. Hurt self and others. Fight, flight, freeze response.	Limit or remove language. One person talks at a time. Distraction. Humour. Act quickly. Offer motivating object/activity. Move to calm space. Change of face – other member of staff takes over. Reassure. Remove others if necessary. Signal that help is needed.
What we may observe What pupil does when in recovery.	**How we can help** Things that we can do to help the pupil once in recovery.
Cry. Be upset. Be remorseful, frustrated or angry. Show feelings of self-loathing, self-doubt and poor sense of self. Panicked that have missed something which is important to him. Panicked about the implications for him. Panicked at how difficult the situation is for him – unable to see a way forward.	Acknowledge and affirm these feelings. Talk to pupil about how the adult can help and what the pupil can do to help himself. Use a comic strip conversation to support understanding of situation and everyone's part in it. Recognise the point at which things went wrong. Reflect on what we could do differently next time (adults and pupil)

Source: Adapted by the author from the STAR and ABC communication analysis chart.

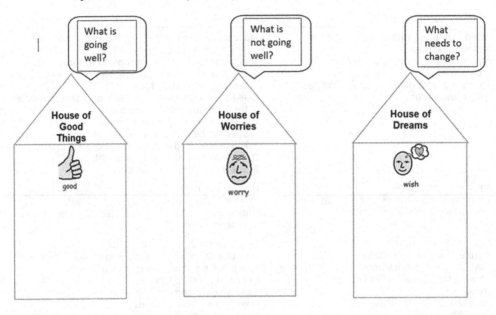

Figure 4.2 The three schools approach.

Adapted by the author from Turnell and Edwards (1999); Weld (2008). Widgit Symbols ©
Widgit Software Ltd 2002-2024 www.widgit.com

The three schools approach

As highlighted in the previous chapter, the three schools template (Weld, 2008; Turnell and
Edwards, 1999) is an easy to use, quick and effective tool to support pupils in sharing their
views, thoughts and feelings of the school. It is a simple tool to support us in generating an
understanding of how our pupils are experiencing school, what is causing anxiety and any
adjustments which they are requesting (Figure 4.2).

Pupil passports

A pupil passport is another tool which can be used to support us in generating an understanding of our pupils. It also supports the pupil to reflect on their strengths and difficulties.
The passport can be used, over time, to support the pupil to consider what they want to
communicate, request any adjustments, consider anything which may or may not be helpful
and request any help which the pupil feels that they may need.

The passport can be useful in generating a discussion between us, the teacher, and the
pupil. This can take place at the end of the year with a teacher who has become very familiar
with the pupil - it can then be shared with a new teacher. It can also be used at the start of
the year as a way of getting to know a new pupil or when something significant has changed
in the child's life. Ideally, the family would contribute to the passport.

The information included in the passport should be presented on a single page. It offers
easily accessible, purposeful and important information about how to support the pupil. The
passport should be easily accessible (and possibly visible) to the pupil and the members of

staff who come into contact with the pupil. It should be considered as a working document which can be managed, updated and adapted by the pupil with increasing independence. It is important that the pupil has an increasing degree of autonomy over their passport so that it becomes a tool which they can use to advocate for themselves.

Different pupil passport templates can be used, dependent on the age, language and maturity of the pupil (Figures 4.3 and 4.4).

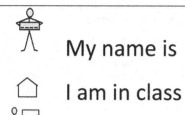 My name is

 I am in class

I like…	I do not like…	You can help me by …
• To meet new friends • To learn English, geography and maps • To play games on the iPad and watch cartoons • To play active games and have fun • Ice cream	• When someone laughs at me • When somebody is rude or says that I am doing or saying things wrong	• Being friendly and nice • Helping me to get around school • Telling me your name • Smiling • Not using jokes or sarcasm

 I can find these things difficult...

1 The one thing that would make the biggest difference to me is

 I am good at..

• Maths and calculations

I can find these things difficult...
• English (both speaking and writing)
• Re-telling stories
• Expessinig my feelings
• Drawing and painting

• When I feel safe (know my routine/timetable) and I'm surrounded by friendly, patient and kind people

Figure 4.3 Example of a pupil passport.

Widgit Symbols © Widgit Software Ltd 2002–2024 www.widgit.com

This is a photo of me

My name is

The things I find difficult are

- English – writing
- I want to be in first place.
- Drawing a real person.
- Making a Sonic statue in Minecraft.
- Focusing in class.

My hopes and dreams

- I would like to be a scientist and to go to Sonic World.

I am worried about

- I'm scared of being on my own at home or at school.
- Getting something wrong in class.
- Strict teacher – I feel like I'm in trouble.

I'm good at I like:

- Games(Nintendo)
- Art
- Winning
- Running
- Sonic
- Pink donuts
- Toy shops
- Kirby games

How you can help me

- Lots of visuals to support.
- Pre-teach / printed flip charts.
- Work in a quiet room.
- The blue room
- Breathing
- Talking
- Playing with putty during input.

What I can do to help myself

- I can ask my learning partner or teacher for help.
- Breathing
- A movement break.

I don't like

- Boring dreams.
- If someone keeps repeating my name.
- Touch
- Shouting/ loud noises.

The one thing that will make the biggest difference to me is

- **Talking about my worries and anxieties.**

Figure 4.4 Example of a pupil passport.

The PATH approach

Another tool which may be helpful in generating an understanding of the pupil, and what is important to them, is the PATH (Planning Alternative Tomorrows with Hope) approach to pupil-centred target and outcome setting (Pearpoint, Forest and O'Brien, 1997; O'Brien, Pearpoint and Kahn, 2015). This directs the pupil to think about an outcome which is desirable to them and supports them to create a number of targets as steps towards this outcome. This tool is most appropriate for pupils who communicate verbally and can be used with pupils of all ages.

In its simplest form, the pupil is asked to think about their dream and asked how we can help, how they can help and how their family can help in realising this dream. The pupil works collaboratively with us to set a goal and a number of targets which are reviewed throughout the year. The following describes the cycle in the English, three term system but could be adapted accordingly.

Autumn term

1. Talk about '**dreams**'. No limits or constraints are placed on the dream so the pupil can indicate what is important to them. Write the dream in the bubble at the top of the Path.
2. From the dream, work with the pupil to come up with a **goal** which can be achieved by the end of the academic year. This may be based on their dream, but it does not have to be.
3. **Now**. Compare the goal with where they are now. Use the prompts to find out: what they would like to get better at; what they need help with; what would make their life better. Ask the pupil to score themselves out of ten. Discuss what success would look like. Do you agree with their score?
4. **Me**. Ask the pupil to identify any strengths that will be useful when working towards their goal and anything that they can do to help themselves (refer to the pupil passport). What will they need to change/do differently? Are they able to make these changes themselves or do they need the support of an adult?
5. Discuss what is already working well and any habits of mind that may be helpful.
6. Talk about access strategies (use the tick sheet discussed in the next chapter) which will help them to achieve their goal.
7. **School**. Ask them how you (their teacher) can help them to achieve their goal. What needs to change/stay the same and who is able to make these changes?
8. **Home**. Ask how their family can help at home.

Spring term

9. **Well Done**. Review progress towards the target. Talk about what is going well, what could be improved and who is responsible. Refer back to the access strategies tick sheet and the pupil passport. Is the goal still relevant? Ask the pupil to score themselves out of ten.

Summer term

10. **Made It**. Discuss whether the pupil has met their goal. Talk about what went well, what could be improved and who is responsible. Refer back to the access strategies tick sheet and the pupil passport. Ask the pupil to score themselves out of ten. Discuss a new goal/next steps.

Table 4.5 The PATH template

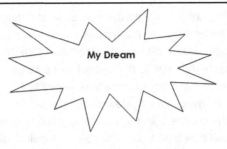

My Dream

Now	Me	School	Home	Well done	Made it	Goal/Reward
I would like to get better at/ need some help with/ barrier to overcome/ what could be better. Score out of 10.	What I need to do/how I can help myself/ what works/ what will make the difference/ thinking skills.	What my teachers can do to help me/ refer to passport/ access strategies.	How people at home can help me.	How am I doing in February? What's going well/What next?Score out of 10.	How am I doing in June? Score out of 10.	Did I make it? Score out of 10.

Source: Adapted by the author from O'Brien, Pearpoint and Kahn (2010).

Resources

- PATH template
- Pupil Passport
- Access strategies tick sheet (discussed in subsequent chapter) (Table 4.5)

Pupil perspectives

The chapter closes with pupils' perspectives on the theme of:

Understand me – I may surprise you

If we are to form a consensus on what an autism-affirming school should be like from the perspective of our pupils, we need to establish that views are commonly held. If many pupils from different schools hold views in common, we can begin to develop an understanding of how autistic pupils are experiencing school and, in turn, begin to consider what an autistic affirming school should be like.

The views of primary-aged pupils, older autistic pupils, and the reflections of adults on their school experience – both primary and secondary have all been considered.

I include quotes from many pupils in several schools, so that their views, thoughts and feelings are recorded verbatim and not paraphrased through an adult. Their narrative serves as a powerful testimony to how they often experience a lack of understanding of themselves as autistic pupils and explains why the implication of the Teachers' Toolbox may be helpful when working towards creating autism-affirming schools.

As well as pupils in my school, the views of pupils in the following schools have been included:

Humphrey and Lewis (2008): 20 pupils across four secondary schools in the north-west of England.

Goodall (2020): 12 pupils from a secondary school in Northern Ireland.

Saggers, Hwang and Mercer (2011): nine pupils form an Australian high school.

Wood (2019): four pupils, three of whom are of primary age. Six autistic adults reflecting on their experience of school – both primary and secondary.

Perhaps surprisingly, pupils form many different schools had experiences in common. A prevalent theme was the feeling that they were often misunderstood by their teachers, friends and peers.

Understand me

Teachers – pupils requested that teachers understand them as an autistic pupil

Teachers' understanding of autism impacted negatively and positively on the pupils' experience of school. The pupils recognised that we, as teachers, had the biggest single impact on their experience of school, both positively and negatively.

Pupils shared experiences of teachers whom they felt did not understand autism or them as autistic pupils:

They do but not enough. They don't understand it enough.

*

All I know is by the way they act they just don't know enough at all.

*

I think the teachers didn't understand me.

*

They don't understand it [autism] enough.

*

By the way they act they just don't know enough [about autism] at all.

*

I don't feel important here.

*

In my old school the teachers were NOT autism friendly.

Goodall reported (2020, p. 95):

I felt like they didn't understand as much as I would have liked them to.

*

Teachers make it [school] worse; they don't understand what I am going through.

*

I was stressed at the teachers because they wouldn't listen to me.

*

> They [bad teachers] are dead inside and don't care about me as a person.

Wood also stated (2019, p. 147):

> Teachers need to understand that they need to attend to us [and] communicate differently. They need to actively listen and learn about us as individuals.

The hope that teachers may improve their understanding of autism was expressed by many pupils.

> Everyone needs to learn more. Everyone needs to be in their science labs, coding on their computers to try and solve the mystery.
>
> *
>
> Well, I would say try and improve your autism knowledge as much as you can and try and learn more about what is the best for the autistic people. Like what type of autism do they have, how should you treat them, what might they feel.
>
> *
>
> If teachers in my old school understood about autism – they could help the children.
>
> *
>
> Learn more about what is best for autistic people.
>
> *
>
> Well, make the teachers understand [about autism].

However, pupils were also able to identify teachers whom they felt had a good understanding of autism.

> They are the ultimate queens of autism. They dig deep, deep, deep into it and let it all out and make me kinda learn a very important lesson.
>
> *
>
> Two teachers don't understand me [the rest do].
>
> *
>
> My class teacher knows about autism.
>
> *
>
> Not really anything that isn't going well with teachers here.
>
> *
>
> Teachers understand about autism.
>
> *
>
> Lovely, funny and not too strict.
>
> *
>
> I like the teachers if they're nice and kind.

Saggers, Hwang and Mercer fed back (2011, p. 179):

> I think it's the feeling where you can talk to them like another student. So you can relate to them, they can relate to you.
>
> *

First of all they'd have to be understanding but firm.

*

Maybe not just treating everyone the same. Thinking of their own strengths and weaknesses and stuff.

Wood added (2019, p. 137):

She understood autism. She was able to know what to do, and because of it, it made the classroom experience enjoyable [and they] liked me because they got to know me, and not my disability.

Understand me

Hidden anxiety - pupils requested that we, their teachers, understand the high level of anxiety which they were working hard to hide

Feelings of anxiety, often due to feeling misunderstood, were reported by many of the pupils.

I feel like a dead bush.

*

All the life has gone out of me.

*

I feel sad.

*

I cry blood when my legs hurt.

*

Worried about bad things happening.

*

I am worried about if I do something wrong or I didn't mean to say something, but I just did it.

*

I'm scared.

The pupils describe how their anxiety is heightened in the classroom as the pressure of work (amount and difficulty) increases. For some pupils, the sensory experience of the classroom, the noise, temperature and the confusion of the teacher's message adds to feelings of anxiety.

The compulsion to hide their anxiety from teachers, friends and peers led to further feelings of distress:

'Cus it's a bit embarrassing going out so I just sit down.

*

I feel scared, and I feel embarrassed.

*

Sometimes I go into the toilet and quietly try and take deep breaths, sometimes I cry in there.

*

I wish I could go in there [the toilet].

*

I stand up, look out of the window and take deep breaths.

*

I tell myself it's going to be ok, and I know that it is.

The pupils felt that a greater understanding on the part of others may lead to a reduction in their anxiety which they felt compelled to hide.

Goodall reported (2020, p. 88):

It was a new piece of pressure each time

*

It was a weight on my shoulders all the time.

*

I always felt stressed, anxious and out of place.

Wood stated (2019, pp.145, 150, respectively):

I had periods of time where I couldn't [speak]. This was usually when I was under great stress.

*

If I am very stressed, my ability to communicate will break down.

Understand me

Friends/peers - pupils requested that their friends and peers understand them and learn more about autism

Pupils also felt it was important that their friends and peers understand about autism generally and get to know them as autistic pupils. Many pupils, especially the older ones, feel that it is important that their peers understand more about autism so that their behaviour is not viewed as 'weird'. Generally, the younger pupils report that they have positive friendships and peer relationships. However, the older pupils report more negative feelings towards friendships and their peers with some reporting feelings of isolation, although others acknowledge friends and peers as a supportive factor, usually when interests are shared.

Everyone needs to learn more.

*

Autism is just something that makes them different to everybody. It's a very special thing to have.

*

A lot of girls make me feel uncomfortable. I want to tell them, but my mum doesn't want me to.

*

Well only if they're really unkind [do children need to understand].

*

I want teachers to know that I am [autistic].

Many of the pupils speak positively about friends and felt that:

[I have] the right amount of friends.

*

[I have] lots of friends.

*

I like to have a catch up with my friends because I do love to talk, I'm a chatterbox, I love to catch up.

*

I'd tell my friends or tell a teacher if I'm feeling sad – they would cheer me up. They make me laugh.

*

They're all my friends.

*

I'm really popular.

*

Playing games with my friends is the best.

*

Play with my friends a lot makes me happy.

*

They're more fun and they like football and I love football. I love football.

*

[I have] good friends.

*

I play with some of my best friends at school and I have six best friends.

*

Well, I had friends which was good.

Rose, aged eight, quoted in Wood (2019, pp.161, 162, respectively):

I am very happy with my friends.

*

Making friends at school I think is important but not the most important thing at school ... because you learn about other people, and maybe get help.

Humphrey and Lewis added (2008, p. 35):

I do have friends who very often stick up for me.

*

Yeah, if people are nice to you, you feel better. When I was in school when people didn't like me, it was rubbish and now many more people like me it's easier.

Other pupils explain that they spend time alone:

> I don't have a best friend. I never feel lonely. Sometimes I am by myself, but I like this.
>
> *
>
> Sometimes I guess [I feel lonely] but no, not really.
>
> *
>
> [I'm] ok by myself sometimes.
>
> *
>
> It [friends] can be both [helpful and unhelpful].
>
> *
>
> I actually play alone but I'm actually fine with that.

However, other pupils report negative and hurtful experiences:

> Friends say they are my friends and I play with them, but I don't like the games.
>
> *
>
> I sometimes don't understand what they're playing and I'm a bit confused about it.
>
> *
>
> I'm not sure who my friends are.
>
> *
>
> They weren't really my friends, they were mean. Because they were mean people.
>
> *

We get on, I think. Well in general like if it was in a new school, I don't really make friends easily. I think I've known them for a long time. I think it's 'cus all of the boys in our class will always play a game together.

(This pupil found the transition to secondary school too overwhelming to manage. I wonder what we could have done differently to ensure that his voice was heard and what adjustments could have been made to facilitate a successful transition to secondary school?)

Saggers, Hwang and Mercer reported (2011, p. 182):

> I've got a sort of semi-friend, although he gets a bit annoyed with me at times.

Goodall also added (2020, p. 94):

> Despite making the effort to be friendly with the ones in my class, I always felt left out and on my own.

Reflections

To what extent do your pupils feel understood as autistic children and young people by their friends, peers and teachers?

Have you asked your pupils to describe the characteristics of a 'good teacher'?

Are you aware of the high levels of anxiety that your pupils are experiencing and are you aware of the most anxiety-provoking parts of the school day?

Are you meeting your pupils 'half-way' or are you expecting them to make adaptations and adjustments, without considering the changes which we need to make?

Summary

As teachers, we feel that we have a good understanding of autism generally and of our autistic pupils specifically. However, as I have highlighted, this may not be the case. Pupils frequently report that their teachers do not understand enough about autism. Overwhelmingly, pupils requested that we generate an insightful and meaningful understanding of autism and of them as autistic pupils. They hope that a greater understanding on our part may make us more aware of the high levels of anxiety which they are working hard to hard from us.

Generating a greater understanding of autism means taking a whole-school approach to creating an inclusive culture where diversity is the norm. This approach recognises the impact of pupil voice, positive autistic identity and self-advocacy, listens to pupils and makes changes to practice which the pupils themselves request. This means recognising the need for generating an understanding on 'both sides' so we can meet our pupils 'half-way' – we should not expect them to do all the running.

Pupils recognise that, as teachers, we have the single biggest impact on their experience of school. The impact can be positive or negative. The approaches described in this chapter may help us to generate a greater understanding of our pupils and in turn make changes to our practice so that we can begin to create autism-affirming schools.

In this chapter, I have:

Considered the theme Understand me – I may surprise you.
Highlighted that although teachers often feel that they have a good understanding of autism, pupils often feel misunderstood by their teachers. This is often resulting in our pupils experiencing high levels of anxiety which they are working hard to hide from us.
Considered how to develop a whole-school, inclusive culture with diversity being the norm, and reflected on autistic identity and pupils' self-advocacy.
Discussed the 'double-empathy' approach and how we can meet our pupils 'half-way.
Explained how we can use pupil voice to support us in developing our understanding of our pupils and explained a number of tools which can support us in this.
The chapter closes with pupils' perspectives on the theme.

References

All Party Parliamentary Group on Autism, The National Autistic Society. (2017). Autism and education in England. https://www.specialneedsjungle.com/wp-content/uploads/2017/11/NAS-APPGA-Education-Report-WEB61390.pdf

Belcher, H. (2022). *Taking Off the Mask*. Jessica Kingsley Publishers.

Bogdashina, O. (2011). Sensory perceptual issues in autism: Why we should listen to those who experience them. *Annales Universitatis Paedagogicae Cracoviensis. Studia Psychologica*, *1*, 145–160.

Brook in Wood, R. (2019). *Inclusive Education for Autistic Children: Helping Children and Young People to Learn and Flourish in the Classroom*. Jessica Kingsley Publishers.

Duffus, R. (2023). *Autism, Identity and Me: A Practical Workbook to Empower Autistic Children and Young People Aged 10+*. Taylor & Francis.

Goodall, C. (2018a). 'I felt closed in and like I couldn't breathe': A qualitative study exploring the mainstream educational experiences of autistic young people. *Autism and Developmental Language Impairments*, *3*, 1–16.

Goodall, C. (2018b). Inclusion is a feeling, not a place: A qualitative study exploring autistic young people's conceptualisations of inclusion. *International Journal of Inclusive Education*. https://doi.org/10.1080/13603116.2018.1523475

Goodall, C. (2020). *Understanding the Voices and Educational Experiences of Autistic Young People: From Research to Practice*. Routledge.

Humphrey, N. and Lewis, S. (2008). Make me normal: The views and experiences of pupils on the autistic spectrum in mainstream secondary schools. *Autism, 12*(1), 23–46.

Milton, D. (2012). On the ontological status of autism: The double empathy problem, *Disability and Society, 27*, 883–887.

National Autistic Society (n.d.-a). Masking. www.autism.org.uk/advice-and-guidance/topics/behaviour/masking

National Autistic Society (n.d.-b). The SPELL framework. www.autism.org.uk/what-we-do/autism-training-and-best-practice/training/the-spell-framework

National Autistic Society. (2023). National Autistic Society Education Report. www.autism.org.uk/what-we-do/news/education-report-2023

O'Brien, J., Pearpoint, J. and Kahn, L. (2015). *The PATH and MAPS Handbook. Person-centred Ways to Build Community*. Inclusion Press.

Pearpoint, J., O'Brien, J. and Forest, M. (2010). *PATH: A Workbook for Planning Positive Possible Futures, Planning Alternative Tomorrows with Hope*. Inclusion Press.

Rowe, A. (2013). *The Girl with the Curly Hair*. Lonely Mind Books.

Saggers, B., Hwang, Y. and Mercer, L. (2011). Your voice counts: Listening to the voice of high school students with autism spectrum disorder. *Australasian Journal of Special Education, 35*(2), 173–190. www.cambridge.org/core/terms. https://doi.org/10.1375/ajse.35.2.173

Sandland, B. (2022). *The Spiral of Self-identification of Autism: Understanding Self-identification of Autism through Firsthand Experiences*. University of Birmingham.

Smith Myles, B. and Southwick, J. (2015). *Asperger Syndrome and Difficult Moments: Practical Solutions for Tantrums, Rage and Meltdowns*. Autism Asperger Publishing Co.

Turnell, A. and Edwards, S. (1999). *Signs of Safety: A Safety and Solution-oriented Approach to Child Protection Casework*. W.W. Norton.

Weld, N. (2008). The three houses tool: Building safety and positive change. In Calder, M. (Ed.). *Contemporary Risk Assessment in Safeguarding Children*. Russell House Publishing.

Willey, L.H. (1999). *Pretending to Be Normal*. Jessica Kingsley Publishers.

Wood, R. (2019). *Inclusive Education for Autistic Children: Helping Children and Young People to Learn and Flourish in the Classroom*. Jessica Kingsley Publishers.

Chapter five

What the pupils said

Help me to understand, understand myself and understand others

Chapter outline

The chapter opens with a discussion on the implications for practice, and consideration of the adaptations and adjustments which were requested by the pupils themselves.

In the Teachers' Toolbox, I suggest strategies which we can use to support our pupils in generating an understanding of themselves as autistic children and young people. I introduce the All About Me programme (Miller, 2018) which supports pupils as they learn about themselves and their own autism. I explain how to deliver the programme and provide the necessary resources for delivery at home or in school. The programme is a strength-based approach to autism which also recognises areas of difficulty and generates an understanding of what autism means to each pupil. I discuss The Zones of Regulation™ framework, an approach to emotional self-regulation based on the original work, *The Zones of Regulation Curriculum* by Leah Kuypers (2011, Inc. All Rights Reserved). I also reflect on the Autism Level Up approach, which supports pupils to explore various aspects of school that may influence their regulation (Laurent and Fede, 2021).

Social stories (Gray, 2015) and comic strip conversations (Gray, 1994) are explained as strategies that may be used to support the pupils in generating a greater understanding of the non-autistic world, something which the pupils themselves requested.

The chapter closes with pupils' perspectives on the theme. The views, thoughts and feelings from many pupils from different schools are included and are recorded verbatim. I explain why the implication of the Teachers' Toolbox may be helpful in creating autism-affirming schools.

Theme and sub-themes

As I have previously highlighted, we should listen to, and act upon, pupil voice if we are to create autism-affirming schools from our pupils' perspective. In this chapter, I consider the theme,

Help me to understand - understand myself and understand others.

DOI: 10.4324/9781003396499-5

The overarching theme is broken down to a number of sub-themes 'underneath' it which focus on different elements of the theme. Each of the sub-themes is notable in that it was mentioned by multiple pupils on several different occasions in a number of different schools.

The theme 'Help me to understand – understand myself and understand others' has two sub-themes:

Themselves – pupils requested support to understand themselves as autistic children and young people.

> Even autistic pupils need to learn more. Even I need to learn more about it. I'm not the king of it.

The non-autistic world – pupils requested support to understand more about the (social aspects of the) non-autistic world.

Wood (2019, p.133):

> I needed a social translator. Even a couple of hints every day would have saved a lot of heartache.

How to support pupils to understand themselves

To support pupils in developing a positive sense of self and understand more about themselves as autistic children and young people it may be helpful to introduce the All About Me programme, which guides the pupil through clearly structured sessions, resulting in their own 'All About Me' booklet (Miller, 2018). The programme uses visual prompts to positively explore the pupil's personality, strengths and interests, areas of difficulty, feelings of difference and what autism means to them. The programme can also be shared with family, friends and peers to support their understanding of the child or young person.

The Zones of Regulation and Autism Level Up frameworks may also be helpful tools in supporting the pupils to generate a greater understanding of themselves, their emotional regulation and energy levels.

The All About Me programme

Pupils requested help to understand themselves as autistic individuals. We should not shy away from talking about their own autism. Discussion may support the pupils to positively embrace their autism and help them to reduce negative feelings, low self-esteem and feelings of self-doubt that feeling different may bring.

In response to pupils requesting a greater understanding of themselves as autistic individuals, we developed the All About Me programme, based on Andrew Miller's book *All About Me: A Step-by-Step Guide to Telling Children and Young People on the Autism Spectrum about Their Diagnosis* (Miller, 2018).

The purpose of the programme is to support the pupils, and their families, through a strength-based approach to understanding themselves as autistic children and young people. For some pupils this involves discussing their autism for the first time; other pupils may know that they are autistic but lack an understanding of what this means to them. For other pupils, the programme can be used to develop an understanding of themselves, and autism is not discussed. The programme can be delivered in school by an adult who knows the pupil well, or resources can be provided for the family to deliver the programme at home. If the family chooses to deliver the programme at home, it is helpful if the school is informed of when this is happening. The programme is a powerful tool to generate an understanding of themselves, something that pupils specifically called for. The programme can also be used with family, friends and peers to support their understanding of the pupil.

Miller started using the All About Me programme in 2004 and has now supported over 250 autistic children and young people through the programme. He reports that over 95 per cent of them responded positively to the programme and found it to be a positive and enjoyable experience overall. Miller suggests that delivering the programme to pupils may have a number of benefits including: protecting long-term emotional wellbeing; supporting the pupils in making informed decisions which affect their lives; generating a better self-understanding and raising self-esteem. Miller found that for some pupils there is a sense of relief and peace of mind in understanding their autism. Other benefits may include: providing an explanation of feeling 'different'; feeling part of a 'club'; developing individual coping strategies; providing much-needed answers; sharing areas of strength and difficulty and removing potential feelings of misunderstanding. It also removes the risk of accidental disclosure to the child, which is more likely to occur as the child gets older.

Miller found that negative outcomes are more likely to occur when the programme is delivered later. However, he also recognises that there are potential downsides to delivering the programme. The programme may have a destabilising effect on the child and their family; it may cause anger towards the person delivering it; it may lead to negative self-perception and feelings of being overwhelmed by the life-long implications of being autistic.

The timing of the delivery of the programme is, therefore, critical and the decision of when the pupil is ready to start the programme (if ever) should always be led by the family. The family should have developed an understanding of (their child's) autism and feel comfortable with it before the programme is introduced. Miller suggests delivering the programme before adolescence and I would concur with this. The child should not feel that something shameful is being withheld from them. In my experience, parents rarely shy away from sharing a diagnosis of dyslexia, developmental co-ordination disorder (dyspraxia) or ADHD with their child.

Support pupils in generating an understanding of the non-autistic world

Over half (51 per cent) of autistic pupils wanted help to understand how to get on with their peers (National Autistic Society, 2023).

Autistic pupils can find it difficult to understand and navigate the social aspects of school. Pupils experience increasingly sophisticated social interactions as they move through school. These social situations may have a series of hidden social rules and it can be difficult for autistic pupils to understand these situations.

51 per cent of pupils reported to the National Autistic Society that they would like to receive help in school to understand how to get on with friends and peers.

Pupils said that they would find it useful if the school provided them with opportunities to develop social skills, in familiar places where they felt comfortable. School could be one of these places and could provide the opportunity for pupils to engage with the social aspects of school life that might otherwise be inaccessible. It is important that, in creating these opportunities, schools are conscious of adapting existing clubs or creating new ones which are adapted to suit the needs of autistic pupils.

Emotional regulation

Emotional regulation is essentially a process that develops over time. It is the capacity to adjust one's emotional and physiological arousal state (energy level) to meet the social, sensory and environmental demands of a situation (Laurent and Fede, 2021).

When pupils are emotionally regulated, they are able to use strategies to shift their emotional state and arousal levels to match and meet the demands of the situation in a way that is helpful to them and enables them to maintain engagement, focus and attention. We may describe this as a well-regulated state. Regulation, therefore, could be described as employing strategies to shift our energy levels and emotions to match the requirements of the situation.

However, when pupils do not have the strategies or tools to adaptively shift their emotion and energy, they may experience an arousal level that is mismatched to the situation (too high or too low). They are, therefore, unable to engage successfully in the situation. This mismatch between their internal energy state and the demands of the situation may be described as emotional dysregulation. Pupils may express this dysregulation through non-verbal communication (behaviour). These behaviours may be labelled as concerning.

To support pupils to be able to maintain a regulated state we need to generate an understanding of the factors which are impacting them. The ABC and STAR frameworks described in the previous chapter may be helpful in this. But as a note of caution, Laurent and Fede (2022) highlight that as non-autistic people, we cannot ever fully know or understand the autistic reality but should aim to understand and validate their experiences.

Social stories and comic book conversations

Social stories and comic strip conversations can support the pupils in their understanding of the non-autistic world but may also be helpful to teachers in generating a greater understanding of their pupils' autistic world.

Social stories and comic strip conversations are social learning tools that support a discussion which should be helpful and meaningful to the pupil (Gray, 2015). They can be used to share information with the pupil that the pupil may be missing or misinterpreting, information that non-autistic individuals usually pick up intuitively. Giving the pupil this additional information can support them in generating their understanding of others, something which the pupils themselves requested.

When working on a social story or comic book conversation, it is critical to recognise that both the autistic and non-autistic perspectives are equally valid. Non-autistic individuals can also use the social story as a tool to generate a greater understanding of the autistic world.

Older pupils may find this approach condescending, especially if it has been used when they were younger. In this case, it may be used with caution if the pupil requests help with a social situation. The situation can then be explored as a series of graphic animations which may be more acceptable to the pupil.

Social stories

A social story should not be used to show the pupil how to behave in a non-autistic manner. It may be used as a tool to support the pupil in generating an understanding of a given social situation to develop their understanding of it. The aim is to help the pupil understand the situation and, therefore, feel more comfortable, safe and empowered when they next encounter the same or a similar situation. It can also support the adult and the pupil to think about what can be done to make the situation easier for the pupil. This may mean the adult making the necessary adaptations and adjustments.

Comic strip conversations

Comic strip conversations (Gray, 1994) can be used to generate an understanding into how the pupil is perceiving a situation. They can be used to support the pupil in developing an understanding of the situation, their part in it and the part of others. Comic strip conversations use stick figures and other symbols to represent social interactions and the abstract elements of conversation. They are essentially simple visual representations of conversations which can support the pupil in their understanding of:

- The things that are actually said in a conversation or social interaction
- The things that are not said in a conversation or social interaction
- How people may be feeling
- What people may be thinking
- What people's intentions may be

By seeing a conversation or social interaction presented visually, the hidden and often unfathomable aspects of the communication (recognising the thoughts, feelings and intentions of others) are visualised and may, therefore, be easier for the pupil to understand.

Teachers' Toolbox

How to support pupils in generating an understanding of themselves

All About Me Programme

Choose a time when the child is emotionally regulated, during a calmer period in their lives, if possible, to introduce the programme. If the child is beginning to ask questions related to their autism, this may mean that they are ready for the programme.

The objectives of the All About Me programme (Miller, 2018) are as follows:

Discover key information about themselves as unique individuals.
Positively introduce the child to autism if they (and their family) are ready.
Provide each child with an individual profile of their strengths and difficulties.

Start a continuous journey of learning to understand themselves as autistic individuals. Contextualise their autism – non-autistic individuals can take adjustments and adaptations to support them and the child can feel empowered to request these.

The programme is a three-step process.

Step 1: Introduce the programme to families.

Begin with sending home a letter to families to invite them to an information session to explain the All About Me programme (Appendix 3). Develop a presentation which explains the programme to the families (Appendix 4). Give all families two questionnaires to complete (please see below) – one for the family and one for the child or young person. Each questionnaire seeks to detail the pupil's understanding of autism in general and specifically related to the pupil. The pupil's questionnaire can be completed in school if the family prefers this. The family also needs to sign a consent form (Tables 5.1 and 5.2).

Table 5.1 Pre-programme child questionnaire

All About Me	
Pre-programme questionnaire for children	
Child's Name: _____	Date: _____
Possible Starter Questions	**Child's Responses**
1. What do you like doing? What are you interested in?	
2. What are your favourite subjects/lessons?	
3. What things are you good at?	

(Continued)

Table 5.1 (Continued)

Question	
4. What things do you find difficult?	
5. How do you feel when you are in busy or noisy places (e.g. lessons where everyone needs to talk or move, in the lunch hall, in assembly)?	
6. Who are your friends?	
7. Do you like break times/lunchtimes? Can you tell me why?	
8. What things make you happy when you are at school (and in other places)?	
9. Do any things upset you when you are at school (and other places)? If so, what are they?	
10. Why do you think you have extra help at school (or elsewhere)?	
11. Do you feel different to other children? If so, in what ways?	

Adapted by the author from Miller (2018).

Adult observation during the meeting

The child's communication:
Child's awareness of their own strengths, differences and needs and willingness to talk about them:
Other observations:

Table 5.2 Pre-programme family questionnaire

All About Me	
Pre-programme questionnaire for the family	
Child's Name: _____ **Date:** _____	
Parent/carer's name: _____	
1. Does your child know that they are autistic? If so, when and what were they told and how did they respond?	
2. Has your child raised questions which may be linked to their autism? If so, what have they asked, said or done?	

(Continued)

Table 5.2 (Continued)

3. Has your child ever told you that they feel different to their friends or peers? If so, what have they asked, said or done?	
4. How does your child prefer to spend their free time? What are their interests and preferred objects?	
5. What are your child's strengths?	
6. What are your child's main challenges associated with their autism?	
7. Do you think that your child is ready to be told about their autism? If not, what preparatory work might be needed?	
8. Would you like your child to participate in the All About Me programme? If so, would you like the programme to be delivered at school or would you prefer to deliver the programme at home?	
9. When do you think would be the best time to start the programme?	
Other relevant information:	

Adapted by the author from Miller (2018).

Step 2: Working through the programme with the pupil to produce an individual booklet.

Start the programme. It is usually delivered across three sessions but could take up to six sessions. Each session is about 30 to 45 minutes' duration. The family is invited and encouraged to attend the session.

The child completes an individual booklet during the sessions, and this forms the structure to the programme (Appendix 5). The pupils can choose to take the booklet home, to share with their family and friends, at the end of the final session.

The All About Me pupil booklet

The booklet starts with the child considering what they look like on the outside, drawing a picture of themselves or taking a photograph of themselves. Next, we use visual prompts to support the pupil to reflect on what they are like on the inside – their personality traits and characteristics (Appendix 6). The pupil uses the cards as prompts to find some words and visuals which describe them. The visual prompts support talking pupils and pupils who use non-verbal communication. There are prompts to support the pupils throughout the programme, reminding the pupils that they are amazing and loved and that their family is proud of them.

The programme moves on to consider the pupil's strengths (Appendix 7) and the things that they find difficult (Appendix 8). To support the pupil with this, a series of strengths and difficulties visual prompt cards are used. The pupils are reminded that everyone finds some things difficult and that this is okay. They are reminded that they may sometimes need help learning to understand other people and that we can help with this. Generally, the first session would finish here. This session can be broken into two sessions, depending on the age and maturity of the pupil.

The family is invited to the second session. Start the second session by asking the pupil to look through the booklet from the first session. If the child is able and willing, ask them to read the booklet out loud.

Proceed with caution. The preparation up to this point should ensure that the pupil has some understanding that they are autistic.

Show the pupil the book, *All Cats Are on the Autism Spectrum* (Hoopmann, 2020), or other books which you feel may be relevant and helpful. Look at the book together and notice that the pupil has characteristics in common with and different to the cats. Talk about each of these characteristics and the cats in general. Give time to the pupil to reflect on why we may be looking at the book. Tell the pupil that all the cats in the book are autistic. Ask the pupil if they have heard of the words autistic or autism and discuss this. If you feel that the pupil is ready, it may be helpful at this point to tell the pupil that they have characteristics in common with the cats because they are autistic too. Ask them how they feel about this and ask them if they have any questions or anything they would like to say. You can use emotion visual prompts to support the child in this. Affirm their autism and reassure them. Tell them that we are all here to help them. Assess any emotional impact on the child and the family.

Finish the session by looking at other autistic people, linking to the pupil's specific interests if possible. Talk about the characteristics of each of these individuals and the positive impact which they have had on society. Tell the child that the next session will be the last session and that next time we meet we will find out more about autism and being autistic. Reassure and affirm.

Start the third and final session by asking the pupil to look through the booklet from the previous sessions. If the child is able and willing, ask them to read the booklet aloud. In this session, we consider what it means to be autistic, reassure the pupil that it is okay to be autistic and explain that their autistic brain works in the same way as some other autistic people's brains. We re-look at things the pupil is good at and enjoys as well as the things they find more difficult. We discuss that autistic people can have special things they are interested in learning about or enjoy doing and can often learn more about these things than people who are not autistic. We stress that this is one of the great things about being autistic. The session finishes with affirming the pupil as a unique individual we are immensely proud of. Give the pupil time for questions and comments before asking whether the pupil would like to take their booklet home. If so, put it in an envelope marked private. Decide whether the envelope is given to the family directly or sent home with the pupil.

Step 3: Understanding the pupil's response to the programme.

Meet with the child to reflect on their response to the programme. Assess whether additional support is needed and put this in place if necessary. Many schools have a highly skilled and specially trained Emotional Literacy Support assistant (ELSA) or Thrive practitioner. They are well suited to offer support to the pupil should it be needed. An ELSA is a trained, school-based learning support assistant whose role is to support the emotional wellbeing of pupils. They are trained by an educational psychologist from whom they receive ongoing group supervision. ELSAs work with pupils to deliver bespoke interventions tailored to the individual need. Thrive practitioners offer a trauma-informed, whole-school approach to improving the mental health and wellbeing of pupils. Older pupils may have access to in-school councillors. Additional support is not generally required.

At the family's request, I have now run the programme with most of our autistic pupils in Year Two to Year Six. In most instances, we have delivered the programme in school, but some families have preferred to deliver the programme at home. We have shared the booklet and the visual prompts with the families to enable this. In line with Miller's (2018) findings, I have found that our pupils responded positively to the programme, and it answered many unanswered questions which they may or may not have voiced. Generally, the pupils were able to identify other pupils who were autistic and took great comfort in this.

I found that friends can be a supportive factor for the pupils and many pupils want to share their autism 'discovery' with their friends and peers. However, peers can also be unaccepting, cruel and judgemental. The challenge is for the school to ensure that pupils have an understanding of autism and neurodiversity. This can be done by ensuring that pupils are immersed in a culture of inclusive diversity as discussed previously in the chapter.

A number of our pupils have chosen to share their diagnosis with their friends and peers, and this has been helpful to them. Pupils share the book *All Cats Are on the Autistic Spectrum* (Hoopmann, 2020) with the class, discussing the cats' Autism characteristics, discussing how the pupils may have some characteristics in common and how these impact on the pupils. We also deliver whole-school assemblies and presentations to individual classes on autism and neurodiversity.

Older pupils may choose to develop an individual All About Me presentation based on the programme using more age-appropriate methods such as Prezi, animation-based presentations or tools widely available on social media platforms.

The Zones of Regulation

Kuypers (2011, p. 3) describes self-regulation as 'the ability to do what needs to be done to be in the optimal state for any given situation', in ways which are supportive to the individual. This includes a pupil developing the ability to regulate their sensory needs, emotions and impulses. As teachers, we should recognise that pupils often do not know what needs to be done and are unable to make the choice which is going to be the most helpful in the situation.

The Zones of Regulation (Kuypers, 2011) is an instructional tool which can be used to support the pupil in generating an understanding of themselves. It teaches the pupil how their emotional regulation, state of alertness, energy levels and impulse control all impact on their levels of engagement and emotional wellbeing. It supports pupils in developing skills which support them in regulating their emotions.

The Zones of Regulation approach offers:
A proactive, skills-based approach to self-regulation.
A simple, common language to understand, talk about and teach self-regulation.
A consistent, metacognitive framework to support pupils in generating an understanding of self-regulation.
A systematic framework which follows a systematic series of lessons.
A flexible and adaptable approach to meet individual pupils' needs.

The four zones

To make it easier for pupils to discuss, consider and begin to understand their feelings, states of alertness, regulation and energy levels are divided into four coloured Zones – Blue, Green, Yellow and Red. The pupils learn to understand more about their emotions and how these are impacting them and their goals and outcomes, throughout the day. The simple, common language and visualisation of these Zones into something concrete and tangible helps the pupils to understand the complex skill of self-regulation and helps adults to support them with co-regulation strategies.

The four Zones of Regulation – Blue, Green, Yellow and Red – are described below. Symbols may need to be used to represent the Zones for our visually impaired and colour-blind pupils.

The four Zones of Regulation™

Based on the original work, *The Zones of Regulation*™ Curriculum by Leah Kuypers 2011.

The **Blue Zone** describes low states of alertness and down feelings, such as when we feel sad, tired, unwell, hurt, lonely or bored. Our energy is low and our body is moving slowly when we are in the Blue Zone.

When in the Blue Zone, we will need to rest and recharge our battery. We can regulate by seeking comfort, resting or re-energising. If we are feeling sad, we will need to be comforted.

The **Green Zone** describes a calm, alert state. We may be feeling happy, focused, content, peaceful or calm. We are ready to learn or play.

We are able to regulate ourselves by using tools and strategies (such as eating a healthy snack, drinking water, exercising, taking a break or going to a calm space) which keep us feeling calm and regulated. These restorative actions help us to proactively help to keep ourselves regulated.

The **Yellow Zone** describes when our energy is higher and our internal state begins to elevate. Our emotions are a little stronger. We may be experiencing stress, frustration, anxiety, excitement, silliness, confusion, nervousness, be feeling overwhelmed or feeling 'fizzy' when in the Yellow Zone.

We will need to take action to regulate our energy levels and feelings as they get stronger. For example, if we are feeling 'fizzy' during a game of football, it may be helpful to take 'time out', remove ourselves from the situation, go and get a drink of water or start some breathing exercises.

Younger pupils will need support from an adult to take affirmative action.

The **Red Zone** describes a state of extremely high energy and intense, very overwhelming feelings. We may be in an extremely heightened state of alertness, potentially triggering our fight, flight, freeze or flee protective response. We may be experiencing feelings of anger, rage, devastation, lack of control, panic or terror.

When in the Red Zone, we may need support to pause to gain a sense of control over our strong feelings and high energy. We are feeling out of control and may be unable to regulate ourselves at this time.

Pupils will need support from an adult to take affirmative action.

The Zones can be introduced to the pupil as a traffic light system. When in the Green Zone, the pupil is good to go; the Yellow Zone signals that the pupil needs to exercise caution and slow down; the Red Zone means stop. The Blue Zone is the rest area where the pupil needs to recharge their battery.

A core principle of The Zones of Regulation is that it is alright to be in any of the four Zones. Pupils will routinely experience different Zones throughout the day. Pupils are supported to understand the behaviours which are helpful to them in each Zone to meet the demands of the situation in a way that is supportive to them. It is important that we do not convey the message to the pupil that the Green Zone is the only acceptable Zone to be in; we should acknowledge, accept, and support the feelings of whatever Zone the pupil is in.

To support the pupils in understanding their self-regulation, they are taught how to recognise a broad range of emotions (their own and others'), develop perspective-taking skills and develop insight into their own triggers. Generating an understanding of how the pupil is experiencing the different Zones throughout the day should enable the teacher to support the pupil in this.

The Zones of Regulation curriculum introduces a 'toolbox' of regulation strategies which we can use to support our pupils' regulation. Pupils are supported to understand the regulation tools that are helpful to them in each Zone to meet their goals and the demands of the situation. Pupils may have a combination of calming, cognitive, alerting and sensory strategies in their toolbox.

A Zones of Regulation support plan can be drawn up collaboratively with the pupil and their family and a toolbox of effective strategies agreed upon. The Zones of Regulation toolbox lists a number of strategies which could support the pupil with their self-regulation. The example below is individual to the pupil (Table 5.3).

A Zones of Regulation toolbox can also list a number of generic strategies which could support a whole class with strategies to support their emotional self-regulation.

Many schools are already using The Zones of Regulation and this also supports pupils in understanding more about the parts of the school day they are finding more difficult. As

Table 5.3 An example of a Zones of Regulation toolbox – individual

My Toolbox			
The BLUE Zone	*The GREEN Zone*	*The YELLOW Zone*	*The RED Zone*
How I am feeling	**How I am feeling**	**How I am feeling**	**How I am feeling**
Sad	Happy	Fizzy	Out of control
Tired	OK	Silly	Angry
Bored	Comfortable	Nervous	Frustrated
Slow	Ready to learn	Uncomfortable	Scared
Unwell	Ready to play	Confused	
What I can do	**What I can do**	**What I can do**	**What I can do**
Drink waterStretch	Notice that I am	Drink water	Remove myself
Shake arms/legs	focused, engaged and	Breathing exercises	Go to my calm space
Stand	ready to learn and	Movement break	Breathing exercises
Go outside	play	Brain break	Use help card
Jump		Use putty	Count slowly
		Talk to an adult	Curl into a ball
		Ask for help	

teachers we can make adaptations and adjustments to support pupils' emotional regulation as we notice how our pupils are experiencing the school day.

Autism Level Up

Laurent and Fede are an autistic self-advocate and an autism advocate who are the co-founders of Autism Level Up. They suggest that we should be endeavouring to understand the (often hidden) factors which are contributing to our pupils' dysregulation (Laurent and Fede, 2021). Recognising and addressing these factors (making adaptations and adjustments) may support our pupils in generating an understanding of the non-autistic world.

Having listened to many autistic voices, Laurent and Fede advocate the use of the concept of energy instead of, or in combination with, the language of emotions. As many autistic advocates acknowledge, emotion words are often difficult for them to access, especially during times of dysregulation. Energy levels may be a more concrete concept which may be more relatable to them.

Laurent and Fede suggest that it may be helpful to focus on understanding regulation as an alignment between the pupil's internal energy state and the energy that is needed for participation in any given situation. We may describe the pupil as well regulated when they and the situation are aligned. This does not necessitate using language related to emotion and may be helpful for some pupils who are not yet able to recognise and label their own emotions.

The approach acknowledges that our pupils often experience dysregulation and mismatches in energy and that this dysregulation requires our support to enable our pupils to develop self-regulation and co-regulation strategies. Self-regulation strategies are those that the child is able to employ on their own. Co-regulation strategies are employed with the support of others. They may involve the pupil responding to the help which is offered by others or involve the pupil asking for help. We should be enabling our pupils to use both strategies.

Having engaged with autistic advocates, Laurent and Fede developed the Energy Meter (Tables 5.4 and 5.5). This is a visual tool designed to support the pupil to generate an understanding of the concept of energy, energy matches and mismatches. The tool may be used to visualise energy matches (a well-regulated state) and energy mismatches (a dysregulated state). The left-hand side (energy needed) is used to record the energy needed to adaptively engage in the current situation. The right-hand side (my energy) is used to indicate the energy level currently being experienced. When the arrows align, the pupil could be described as well regulated and support may not be needed. However, when the arrows are mis-aligned the pupil could be described as dysregulated. There is a discrepancy between the energy needed to function adaptively in the situation and the pupil's current energy levels and regulatory strategies will be needed to support the pupil to re-regulate.

The Energy Meter could be used as a tool to support the pupil to visualise this energy mismatch and may be helpful in supporting their understanding that they need to engage in regulatory strategies to help them to match their energy levels to the situation.

We should be mindful of the risk factors which increase our pupils' susceptibility to dysregulation. The risk factors are different to those affecting non-autistic pupils and will vary for each pupil.

Table 5.4 An example of The Zones of Regulation™ toolbox – whole class

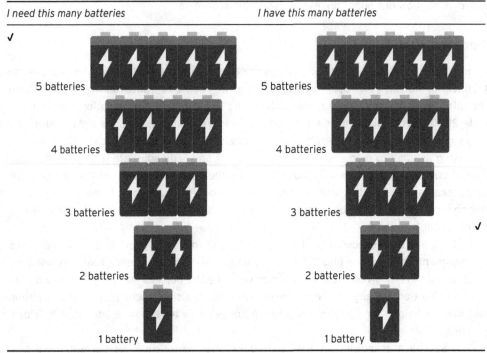

Smashicons, FreePik.

Table 5.5 The Energy Meter

When	What do I need to do?	How much energy do I have? 1–10	How much energy do I need? 1–10	How much energy will I have left?	What do I need to do?	How much energy do I have now?
Start of the school day	Registration	10	5	5	Re-energise Drink of water Deep breathing Read + 2	7
Lesson 1	English	7	7	0	Movement break + 3	3
Lesson 2	Maths	3	2	1	Break – time alone +5	6

Adapted by the author from Laurent and Fede (2021).

Social stories

How to write a social story

The teacher or other adult takes on the role of the author of the story but the child is the subject of the story (Gray, 2015). The author begins with gathering information which will hopefully lead to uncovering the difficulty which the pupil is experiencing in the situation. The author can then develop a personalised story to support the pupil in understanding and overcoming the difficulty. The social story should have a purpose for the pupil. For example, the purpose may be to teach the pupil to leave the building when a fire alarm sounds.

Begin with gathering information about the situation which the pupil is finding difficult or anxiety-provoking. The content and presentation of the story should be appropriate to the child's age and maturity. Photographs, picture symbols and drawings with text can all be helpful.

When gathering information, it may be helpful to think about the story answering six questions: where, when, who, what, how and why?

Consider:
Where the situation occurs.
When the situation occurs.
Who is present.
How it begins and ends.
How long it lasts.
Frequency of the situation.
What actually happens in the situation.
Why the situation is happening.

Also consider whether the situation and/or the outcome of the situation are guaranteed? Is it necessary to use words like sometimes, often or usually?

Personalise the story

Stories should appeal to the interests of the child and wherever possible the child should understand that it is important that they generate an understanding of the situation. It should use non-anxiety-provoking, gentle and supportive language which the child can understand. It should be made up of descriptive sentences and coaching sentences. Directive sentences may also be necessary; you may need to be directive to keep the child safe from harm.

A descriptive sentence accurately describes the context, such as where the situation occurs, who is there, what happens and why. For example:

- The first day of term is 1 September.
- At school, the fire alarm may sound. The fire alarm makes a loud noise which hurts my ears. Usually, when the fire alarm sounds it is a practice. This means that there is not a fire. The fire alarm sounds so that we can practise what we need to do if there is a fire. The fire alarm sounds to keep us safe.

A coaching sentence gently guides behaviour, for example:

- It is ok to ask an adult for help.
- When I feel angry, I can take three deep breaths, go for a movement break or go to my calm place.

A directive sentence gives a specific instruction, for example:

- When I hear the fire alarm, I must leave the building and go straight to the playground. I can take my ear defenders with me.

How to use social stories

Consider how often and who will share the story with the pupil.

Share the story with the child when everyone is feeling calm and relaxed. Do not include any words which may trigger the child. For example, I have written a special story for you. It is about loud noises. Let's read it together now. If the sound of the fire alarm is a trigger for the child, do not mention the word 'alarm' when suggesting that you share the story.

Reflect on how the story is received and whether it is having the desired impact.

Tackle one situation at a time so the child does not feel overwhelmed. Prioritise the situations from the child's perspective; start with what is most important to the child.
The pupil should have an autonomous role in the story.
The story should not be used to teach the pupil how to respond in situations.
Offer choices to guide the child and to support their understanding of the situation.
Initially, use the social story to discuss a situation which is familiar to the child.

Social Stories: Remember

Be **descriptive**: describe where, who, what and why. Where is the social situation likely to happen, who is likely to be involved, what is likely to happen and why.
Be **prescriptive**: describe the likely reactions, thoughts and feelings of the other people who are likely to be present.
Be **directive**: state the responses which may be/are helpful for the child.

Comic strip conversations

How to use comic strip conversations

When introducing a comic strip conversation for the first time, start with a situation which the pupil understands (Gray, 1994). This will support the pupil in becoming familiar with the concept of representing a social interaction visually using stick figures and other symbols. When the pupil is comfortable with the concept of 'drawing conversations', you can begin to use comic strip conversations to reflect on situations which the pupil finds difficult or situations which have not gone well for the pupil.

The following is a guide of how to work through a comic strip conversation with a pupil.

- Initiate a non-threatening conversation with the pupil.
- Gently steer the pupil and begin to discuss the situation which they have found difficult.
- Draw the conversation as the pupil is talking.
- Summarise the situation you have discussed using the drawings as a guide.

- Identify the point at which the situation or interaction went 'wrong' for the pupil or from the pupil's perspective.
- Think together about what everyone could have done differently at this point and whether these actions would have led to a different outcome. The purpose is not to make the pupil feel that they have done something wrong but to generate an understanding of the situation for the pupil. The adult can also develop an understanding of how the child was feeling and what they were thinking in the situation.
- Develop an action plan for similar situations in the future.
- It may be helpful to number the drawings in the sequence in which they occurred.

I am not suggesting that all these tools are implemented; I have included a selection of things which may be helpful. Different tools will be more helpful for some pupils in some settings.

Pupil perspectives

The chapter closes with pupils' perspectives on the theme of:

Help me to understand - understand myself and understand others.

If we are to form a consensus on what an autism-affirming school should be like from the perspective of our pupils, we need to establish that views are commonly held. As I have highlighted, if many pupils from different schools hold views in common, we can begin to develop an understanding of how our autistic pupils are experiencing school and, in turn, begin to consider what an autism-affirming school should be like.

I include quotes from many pupils in several schools, so that their views, thoughts and feelings are recorded verbatim and not paraphrased through an adult. Their narrative serves as a powerful testimony to how they often experience a lack of understanding of themselves as autistic pupils and explains why the implication of the Teachers' Toolbox may be helpful when working towards creating autism-affirming schools.

As well as pupils in my school, the views of pupils in other schools have also been included. Perhaps surprisingly, pupils form many different schools had experiences in common. A prevalent theme was the feeling that they would like support to understand what autism means to them and requested support to generate a greater understanding of the non-autistic world.

Help me to understand

Themselves - pupils requested support to understand themselves as autistic children and young people.

Pupils requested a greater understanding of themselves as autistic pupils. They said that they would like support to understand themselves as autistic individuals and understand their own autism. Many pupils, especially the older ones, felt that it was important that they understood more about autism and what autism meant for them:

> And it's nearly as important for children because if they don't know they are autistic some people might be doubting themselves. Like what I used to do in Year

> 4 and 3. I doubted myself and thought why am I so weird, what's going on? Then
> you learn about autism, and you learn about your actions and some people can do
> really well achieving their goals.
>
> *

When I was in Year 1, I was a terror, a terror, I was screaming but now I've improved. It's taken me five whole years to do it, over a thousand days and I've become a lovely, happy, handsome boy. One pupil, who had been given a positive narrative of autism, viewed his autism as:

> A very special thing to have.

And others said:

> I want to be myself and be amazing. I don't really care what people think of me, but I
> love being myself.
>
> *

He's [an autistic friend] one of the brightest kids I know. And I bet he's going to achieve lots and people have to dig down and reach their full potential, nearly what he has done. And that's what I'm trying to be doing. I don't know if I've reached it yet, probably not but something tells me that I'll soon hit the top level. And soon I'm going to be in secondary school and improve even more.

Wood (2019, p. 84):

> The important things. Learning about ourselves and learning how to be happy.

Help me to understand

The non-autistic world – pupils requested support to understand more about the social aspects of the non-autistic world.

Pupils who participated in social communication learning generally saw it as an effective way of enabling an understanding of their own autism as well as giving an insight into how others (autistic and non-autistic) experienced the world. Pupils felt that this could be effective in generating an understanding of the non-autistic world and support others in understanding the autistic world.

> I wouldn't say it's the funest thing but it's still good.
>
> *
>
> Like social learning, it helps me.
>
> *
>
> I really like that. It's fun and I love it, I love it
>
> *
>
> Social learning is going well.

Wood (2019, p.154):

> The difficulties I encounter are due to others not understanding or not being will-
> ing to understand.
>
> *

Non-autistic people seem to have ... quite rigid ways of communicating.

Pupils were able to articulate how it helped them:

YES, IT DOES. It helps me to calm down, relax, so I can keep on having a good day.

*

Helps me being more flexible.

*

I have learnt more to help me.

*

I've got it today. I don't know why but my fizziness is up the ceiling, I have no clue why. But I'm so fizzy, I could ping around for hours. But it helps me to get into the green zone and relax.

*

[I've learnt] to be a good [social] detective.

*

Helps me to stretch my brain and make me feel comfortable.

*

Helps me in the way it's supposed to help me; being more flexible with decisions.

*

Learnt about asking questions, I can do it now.

*

Sometimes help me solve my problems. Sometimes get me to sort this out myself when I don't really want to.

*

I've learnt that you don't actually go up to people you don't know and stop them and say, 'you look nice' and I was like oh I didn't know that.

Saggers, Hwang and Mercer (2011, p. 181):

We also do this social skills which helps us.
It's sometimes not curriculum or stuff like that I need help with. It's maybe just personal stuff, which is good. It also helps ... and we also do this social skills which helps us socialise.

Reflections

Are your pupils aware of their autism diagnosis?

What do your families feel about their child's diagnosis?

Are families aware of other autistic children and young people?

What are you doing to support your pupils in generating an understanding of themselves as autistic children and young people?

Have you used social stories or comic strip conversations to help your pupils generate an understanding of the non-autistic world?

Are you aware of how you are moving in and out of different Zones of Regulation™ throughout the school day?

Summary

Pupils request support to understand themselves as autistic children and young people. A way of supporting pupils to generate a greater understanding of this may be to introduce the All About Me programme. The approach has been used with hundreds of autistic pupils and is well received by pupils and their families.

Many schools are already using The Zones of Regulation and this also supports pupils in understanding more about the parts of the school day which they are finding more difficult. As teachers we can make adaptations and adjustments to support pupils' emotional regulation as we notice how our pupils are experiencing the school day.

Support to understand more about the social aspects of the non-autistic world was also requested by pupils. Using social stories and comic strip conversations may help the pupil with this and may also support us in generating a greater understanding of how our pupils are experiencing school, particularly the social aspects.

Pupils recognise that generating a greater understanding of themselves as autistic children and young people and of the non-autistic world would have a positive impact on their school experience. The approaches described in this chapter may help us to support our pupils in generating an understanding of the autistic and non-autistic worlds. Introducing these approaches to our practice may be helpful as we begin to create autism-affirming schools.

In this chapter, I have:

Considered the theme: help me to understand – understand myself and understand others.
Suggested various strategies and approaches to support pupils in generating an understanding of themselves as autistic children and young people.
Introduced tools that may be used to support the pupils in generating a greater understanding of the non-autistic world.
The chapter closes with pupils' perspectives on the theme.

References

Gray, C. (1994). *Comic Strip Conversations: Illustrated Interactions that Teach Conversation Skills to Students with Autism and Related Disorders: Improving social … and Other Developmental Disabilities.* Future Horizons.

Gray, C. (2015). *The New Social Story Book, Revised and Expanded 15th Anniversary Edition: Over 150 Social Stories that Teach Everyday Social Skills to Children and Adults with Autism and their Peers.* Future Horizons.

Hoopmann, J. (2020). *All Cats Are on the Autism Spectrum.* Jessica Kingsley Publishers.

Kuypers, L. M. (2011). *The Zones of Regulation: A Curriculum Designed to Foster Self-regulation and Emotional Control.* Think Social Publishing, Inc.

Laurent, A. C. and Fede, J. (2021). Leveling up regulatory support through community collaboration. *Perspectives of the ASHA Special Interest Groups,* 6(2), 288–305. https://doi.org/10.1044/2020_persp-20-00197

Miller, A. (2018). *All About Me: A Step-by-step Guide to Telling Children and Young People on the Autism Spectrum about Their Diagnosis.* Jessica Kingsley Publishers.

National Autistic Society. (2023). National Autistic Society Education Report www.autism.org.uk/what-we-do/news/education-report-2023

Wood, R. (2019). *Inclusive Education for Autistic Children: Helping Children and Young People to Learn and Flourish in the Classroom.* Jessica Kingsley Publishers.

Chapter six

What the pupils said
Hide support for me, or I won't use it

Chapter outline

The chapter opens with a discussion on the implications for practice, and consideration of the adaptations and adjustments which have been requested by pupils themselves. I discuss the pupils' perspectives on the overarching theme and each of the five sub-themes: the sensory classroom and school environment; learning and the curriculum; teachers' understanding of the support that is needed; unstructured times (break time and lunch time); and home learning/homework. The sub-themes are elements of the school experience that are impacting on the pupils' experience of school.

In the Teachers' Toolbox, I include several strategies which may support teachers in their understanding of the support which the pupils themselves have requested and how to deliver this support, skilfully and subtly. These include a classroom checklist, access strategies and visual communication resources.

The chapter closes with pupils' perspectives on the theme. I include quotes from several pupils from different schools, so that their views, thoughts and feelings are recorded accurately and not interpreted by adults. Their narrative serves as a powerful testimony to how the pupils often experience a lack of understanding of the support which they need, how this support is offered and delivered and the adaptations which they found helpful. I explain why the implication of the Teachers' Toolbox may be helpful in creating autism-affirming schools.

Themes and sub-themes

As I highlighted in previous chapters, three key themes emerged, from listening to pupils, which it may be helpful to listen to and act upon if we are to create autism-affirming schools from the pupils' perspective. The themes, 'Understand me – I may surprise you' and 'Help me to understand – understand myself and understand others', were discussed in the previous chapters.

The third theme which emerged from conversations with pupils was 'Hide support for me – or I won't use it'. To aid our understanding of the pupils' perspectives, this overarching theme has been broken down to a number of sub-themes 'underneath' it. The sub-themes focus on different elements of the overarching theme. The theme Hide support for me – or I won't use it has five sub-themes. Each of the sub-themes is notable in that it was mentioned by multiple pupils on several different occasions. Each of the sub-themes will be discussed in detail in this chapter.

DOI: 10.4324/9781003396499-6

The third theme, 'Hide Support for me – or I won't use it', has five sub-themes.

The classroom environment – pupils requested adaptations and adjustments to the sensory environment.

> Places to sneak into for a few seconds. It would be perfect.

Learning and the curriculum – pupils requested flexibility in how the curriculum is delivered.

> And I'd say slow down the work. I think that's really it.

Teachers – pupils requested that teachers understand the support that they needed and how to deliver it with subtlety and skill.

> Saggers, Hwang and Mercer (2011, p 181): 'I sort of feel a bit well, just different, when I'm just the one getting help.'

Unstructured times – break- and lunchtimes were sometimes difficult for the pupils.

> I'd like to go to a quiet place – lots of lunchtimes. Go with friends. With computers and lots of board games – like Cluedo.

Homework – most pupils found this stressful and anxiety-provoking

> It's terrible in my opinion, terrible.

Implications for practice

The third theme, hide support for me – or I won't use it, is inextricably linked to the themes discussed in the previous chapters. Despite our best endeavours, we may lack understanding of the factors which are impacting on our pupils, the support that they may, or may not need, and how this support should be offered and delivered in a way which is acceptable to our pupils.

The National Autistic Society school survey (2023) reported that a considerable number of parents thought that important adaptations or adjustments had not been made to facilitate their child's learning. The Society asked parents to report on the extent to which a variety of reasonable adaptations and adjustments had been made, such as a quiet room or the way tasks were explained. Across every type of adjustment, **the most common answer was that the adjustment had not been made at all**. Parents felt more could be done to create more supportive learning environments within autism-affirming schools.

Autistic children and young people reported similar levels of dissatisfaction. Just over half (53 per cent) of the autistic children and young people who responded to the most recent National Autistic Society School Report said they have someone they can go to if there is a problem. A similar number (48 per cent) said that they have a quiet space to go to or have extra time to do their work. Yet, there is a clear demand for these adaptations and adjustments. More than half (54 per cent) of autistic children and young people expressed a strong desire to use quiet spaces more often, particularly during break times when they recognised their need for a safe/quiet space.

We can use our pupils' perspectives to help us to generate an understanding of our part in the dynamic relationship between our pupils and their experience of school. Pupils understand that it is us, as teachers, who have the single biggest impact on their experience of school. Pupils ask that we consider the impact that the sensory environment, learning and the curriculum, teachers' understanding of the support which is needed, unstructured times and home learning/homework is having on them. Arriving and leaving school may also be a factor for some of our pupils. Therefore, it is important that we understand how each of these factors (and there may be others) is impacting our pupils, positively or negatively.

Consider which of these factors is having the greatest impact on our pupils and how the dynamics of the relationship between the pupil and each of these factors will change whenever we alter one of the factors.

Think about the anxiety which our pupils experience when any one of these factors goes wrong or is changed.

Our pupils need to feel assured that the adaptations and adjustments, which they need to manage the impact of each of these factors, are in place and that these are available consistently, whenever they are needed. The more explicit we are about the support that is in place, the more helpful this is for our pupils.

Consider which of these adjustments are non-negotiable as part of a whole-school approach:

Learning environments without superfluous visual distractions.
Visual timetables in all classrooms, referred to throughout the day.
Class timetables and schedules adhered to and on display in the classroom.
Any change communicated explicitly to the pupils.
Unconditional access to safe/quiet spaces in and out of the classroom available.
Ear defenders, sensory cushions and 'concentration screens' made available.
Written instructions available.
Instructions given clearly and succinctly with key words emphasised.
Models and worked examples on display in the classroom.
Visual and concrete learning resources made available and signposted.
Clearly communicated expectations about the quantity and quality of learning expected.
Communication of when the task or lesson is 'finished'.
Access to a quiet place at break and lunch times.
Flexible home learning/homework stipulations.

We also need to recognise that our pupils may want the adaptations and adjustments to be delivered subtly and skilfully so that their friends and peers are not aware of them. It is incumbent on us, as teachers, to ensure the necessary support and adaptations are in place. When we generate a greater understanding of this, we will be able to support our pupils in ways that are acceptable and helpful to them.

How can the adaptations and adjustments, which our pupils request, be kept hidden from friends and peers?

Pupils requested that we generate a greater understanding of the adaptations and adjustments they need to cope with the factors which are impacting them (the sensory experience of the classroom; the increasing pace, amount and difficulty of learning and the curriculum; break- and lunchtimes and the demands of home learning/homework). They requested a greater understanding of how support with each of these is offered and delivered. The pupils acknowledged that they needed additional support but may reject this if it is not delivered in a way which is acceptable to them. They requested that support is delivered subtly and not to them exclusively. They were very firm in their belief that we do not always understand the anxiety that they are experiencing, and a lack of support or clumsily delivered support can add to this anxiety. Rejecting the help which is needed is likely to heighten our pupils' feelings of stress and anxiety.

Pupils are able to identify adjustments to practice which would lead to a more positive school experience. These adjustments could help to alleviate feelings of anxiety, which the pupils are working hard to hide, improve their experience of school and lead to better outcomes. The adjustments requested by the pupils would usually be beneficial to all pupils in the school and would certainly not be detrimental to them.

I will now describe the adaptations and adjustments which pupils requested to the sensory environment, learning and the curriculum, us as teachers, unstructured time and homework

The classroom and school environment

The difficulty of managing the sensory classroom and the school environment is expressed by many pupils. Pupils report that they are affected negatively by the sensory and physical environment of the classroom and that this causes them undue stress and anxiety.

It is a commonly held misconception that if the pupils are learning in a well-ordered classroom environment, with good behaviour management and positive attitudes to learning, the pupils will not experience difficulties with the sensory environment. This is not the case. Focus and attention in the classroom are impacted negatively by the sensory experience and many pupils report that they also find it hard to manage the playground, the lunch hall and transitions between lessons and around school. Pupils often find the classrooms noisy, hot and cramped, with not enough space. Many pupils describe their hyper-sensitivity to everyday sensory inputs which most pupils are not aware of or can easily tune out from. Sounds such as a humming projector or a ticking clock are overwhelming for some pupils. Other pupils describe difficulties in filtering out superfluous and unhelpful information so that they are able to focus and attend to the relevant and helpful parts. Some of our pupils will only to able to switch on one sensory channel at a time. They may be able to listen to us but are unable to look at or towards us at the same time. Some pupils may be able to listen when they are on the periphery or look at you with peripheral vision. This is exhausting for our pupils and will impact on their focus and attention, sometimes resulting in shutdown with obvious impacts on learning.

Bogdashina recognises that 'a breakthrough [in our understanding of how autistic people are experiencing the sensory world] has come from the personal accounts of people on the autistic spectrum' as we may have previously described our pupils' experiences from the outside rather than how it feels from the inside' (Bogdashina, 2011, p. 145). She suggests that instead of questioning why our pupils behave the way they do, we should be trying to generate an understanding of how they experience and perceive the world.

As teachers, we should be aware of how our pupils' sensory experience can significantly impact on their ability to focus, attend and stay regulated within the classroom and the school environment. Each pupil will have an individual and unique experience of the sensory environment. Their experiences will differ from each other in the same way as their non-autistic peers. Responses to the sensory environment, which may seem unusual to us, are logical, functional and helpful for our pupils. From our pupils' perspective, these responses are 'normal' and are not necessarily difficulties which cause the pupils problems. Bogdashina recognises that some of our autistic pupils may have 'superabilities' which non-autistic people are unable to appreciate as we do not know that they exist and are not able to experience them. (Bogdashina, 2011, p. 149). We should recognise that we may not be able to understand these as we have no experience of them.

Therefore, the only way to understand and meet a pupil's sensory needs is to discuss with them how they are experiencing the environment and make every effort to put in place the adaptations and adjustments which they would find helpful and have skilfully developed in order to cope.

That said, there are a number of adaptations and adjustments which were requested by many pupils. Most pupils requested breaks inside and outside the classroom, to give them time in a quiet/safe place with fewer people around them. Pupils recognised that a short period of time spent outside the classroom is helpful and a short break is often all that they need to re-regulate. Having access to a safe/quiet space, at any time throughout the day, must be unconditional, should be planned for and discussed with the pupil, and should not draw the attention of their peers. This can be facilitated by a non-verbal cue, a visual sign or an agreed verbal cue.

Moving around the school at different times, going to lunch early, eating in a quieter place, avoiding busy morning and afternoon transitions, avoiding the playground and coming to school through a quieter entrance are helpful strategies requested by some pupils.

While ear defenders are requested by some, others were uncomfortable with the visibility of wearing them. It may be helpful to have ear defenders commonly available to more pupils (especially in the lunch hall) although there may be hygiene issues around this. Some older pupils prefer using ear plugs as these are more discrete and peers are not aware of them.

Pupils often had clear views about their preferred seating position. Pupils may prefer to sit at the front to limit distractions, however, others may request a place at the back, where they know that no one is behind them, or at the side near a window or door. Some pupils report that they find it difficult to manage the close proximity of other pupils. In this case, a 'concentration station' or 'quiet corner' may be helpful, where they can sit away from other pupils when they need to focus and attend independently to a learning task. Some pupils find 'low arousal screens' helpful and find this to be a helpful tool to minimising sensory input. **Talk about these adaptations and adjustments with your pupils to determine which may be helpful**, being mindful that these strategies should be offered as a choice and not enforced.

Learning and the curriculum

Learning and the curriculum is another element that pupils describe impacting negatively on them. Although every pupil's experience of learning and the curriculum is different, as with the sensory environment, pupils do hold views in common, with many pupils finding the demands of the curriculum overwhelming and stressful, especially as the amount, difficulty and the pace of the learning increases, as they move through school. Pupils in Year Six also expressed feeling stressed by the thought of completing the Standard Assessment Tests (SATS) at the end of the year.

Many pupils express a preference for practical and factual subjects, with reduced demands for writing, while activities that involve writing at length are generally less popular. Many perceive the demand for writing as a significant difficulty and this impacts on their enjoyment of parts of the curriculum which involve writing at length, especially in English. They find writing physically demanding and exhausting. English may also be perceived to involve more collaboration and discussion which may be more challenging for some pupils.

Pupils feel that they could be supported to write when necessary and allowed to respond, as succinctly as possible, at other times. Consider whether the pupil could demonstrate their understanding of a concept in a way that means they do not need to write down an answer. Perhaps pupils could be provided with opportunities to show knowledge and understanding of concepts in ways that require little or no writing by enabling access to voice to text, typing, programmes which support writing, cutting and sticking activities, responding to multiple choice questions, shared writing and so on.

When pupils are required to produce an extended piece of writing, they request help in structuring the work, and access to visual prompts such as writing frames, mind maps, word banks, stem sentences and so on. Offering visual scaffolds may help to reduce the anxiety around extended pieces of written work. Remember, we should not be offering these exclusively to a pupil as this can generate negative feelings of difference.

Pupils request that learning should be broken down into carefully sequenced learning steps so that they can see how they are progressing through the learning task. Many also ask for concrete resources and visual scaffolds to support them to complete the task. Pupils said that concrete maths resources, models, worked examples displayed on working walls or examples of finished work are all helpful.

All pupils benefit from repetition and consolidation of previous learning, and it is helpful to all pupils if concepts are revisited before new learning is introduced. Some pupils recognise that they need additional time to process information and acquire new learning, especially when learning a new or unfamiliar concept. This means that the pupils may need longer to complete learning tasks or may need to revisit the concept more often. We can support our pupils by giving them the same level of challenge but enabling them to move through it by removing the need to record superfluous information. We may consider the number of questions which the pupil needs to complete to demonstrate their understanding. Pre-teaching, post-teaching and over-teaching may also be helpful.

We can also support pupils by offering visual prompts to support them when they need help and ensure that they have the tools to ask for help when they need it. These could include traffic light templates, task planners, previously agreed methods of non-verbal communication or help cards. We should not assume that if a pupil is not putting up their hand and asking for help, they do not need it.

Some pupils report that responding to questions in front of the class is stressful. As teachers, we should know which pupils need to be pre-warned of a question and understand the length of time the pupil may need to process the question and formulate a response. This may be several seconds.

It is important that we know which are our pupils' preferred subjects. Pupils should not be removed from preferred subjects to catch up on the parts of the curriculum which they find the most difficult. This is unfair and demotivating.

Finally, remember that pupils report that they want support with their learning (especially with English and subjects which require extended written responses) but they do not want this support to be offered to them exclusively.

Teachers and how support is offered and delivered

As I highlighted in previous chapters, as teachers we have the biggest positive and negative impact on our pupils' experience of school. I have already highlighted that many pupils feel that as teachers, we do not understand them as autistic pupils and do not recognise that they are experiencing high levels of stress and anxiety at school.

The compulsion to hide this anxiety from us leads to further feelings of distress amongst our pupils. Pupils are working hard to hide the fact that they need support and the rejection of support is often resulting in unnecessary stress and negative experiences of school. Pupils recognise that they need support (with learning and the curriculum, self-regulation, the sensory experience of the classroom) but they will often reject this support if they feel that it is offered to them exclusively or clumsily. Teachers are incorrect in believing that if our pupils reject support, it is because the support is not needed. This is not the case.

Pupils are able to share their perspectives on the support which they need but may only accept support if it is hidden from their peers or delivered subtly and skilfully by a trusted adult. Pupils report that they may feel too embarrassed to use the supportive strategies or adaptations which have been put in place to help them and prefer to hide their need for these from us. This is often at great detriment to themselves.

As teachers, we play a crucial role in our pupils' emotional responses to school. An insightful and understanding teacher offering support skilfully and subtly will have a positive impact on the pupil. Pupils reported that they need to feel safe at school and understand that their teacher can be a safe and trusted adult who understands and supports them with their feelings of anxiety, their learning and self-regulation. We can use the tools described in the previous chapters to recognise and understand situations which are likely to be anxiety-provoking for our pupils and, if possible, reduce the pressure of other factors in these situations. For example, collaborative working is important in the classroom, but we should recognise that the increased noise and close proximity to peers at these times, together with a possible lack of social understanding, may be difficult for some of our pupils. The need for additional time out of the classroom before, during or after collaborative working may be necessary. Pre-warning of the task and the expectations around it may also be helpful.

Many pupils said that members of support staff are helpful and even older pupils recognise that this support may be beneficial. This may be because these members of staff are trusted by the pupils and understand the pupils' need for the subtle and skilful delivery of support. We know that some pupils do not want their peers to be aware that they need anything different from their peers. Therefore, it may be easier for a pupil to ask for help from a member of support staff who is close by, rather than asking the class teacher, as this request for help may be more visible and obvious to their peers. It is important that we, therefore, notice the support which the pupil may need, offer this skilfully and subtly, are close enough that we can be called upon when necessary or we have a visual support system in place, so the pupil is always aware that there is someone who is available to help. These strategies are more important when we are working in a classroom without a member of support staff.

As I have highlighted, some pupils said that they would prefer that their requests for additional support were invisible to their friends and peers. This was particularly important when requesting to leave the classroom for a brain, movement or sensory break. As I have already mentioned, pupils want access, throughout the day, to a quiet/safe space as this helps them to manage their feelings of anxiety and supports their emotional regulation. Pupils mention the need for this more often as they move through the school and during periods of dysregulation.

Predictability and routine and structured learning environments, with reduced distractions, are important to our pupils and helpful in relieving feelings of anxiety that they may be feeling. Pupils request weekly and daily visual timetables, with advance warning of change and describe how they rely on visual timetables displayed in classrooms to manage the school day.

Visual timetables support our pupils by using visuals, symbols and words to represent the main activities of the day, in the order in which they are happening. It may be helpful to have a simple visual timetable on display in every classroom in the school. As each activity is completed, remove the visual symbol from the timetable so that the pupil can see that the activity is 'finished'. Introduce the timetable at the start of each day and after lunch and refer to the timetable throughout the day. As pupils request advance warning of change, it is important to have a visual cue to indicate any change to routine and talk to the pupils about planned, unplanned, expected and unexpected changes. We can symbolise change by using a 'whoops' or change symbol. When supporting our pupils to accept a change to the timetable, it is helpful to change from a less desirable to a more motivating activity. This supports them in their understanding that change can be positive.

For many of our pupils, a whole-class visual timetable is enough to help them to understand the daily routine and to prepare them for change. However, some may find it helpful to have an individual timetable which they have autonomy over. This can be on their table, at their 'concentration station' or on the wall, at their height near to where they sit. The pupil should be supported on how to use the timetable independently.

Some of our pupils may also benefit from a 'now and next' board. This supports them to understand what is happening now and what is going to happen next. It can support pupils who are having difficulties engaging in less-preferred learning tasks by showing them that something more motivating is coming next. The pupil may need support to understand that they need to finish the activity, which is happening now, before they can do the next activity. It may be helpful to use visual timers alongside the now and next board so the pupil understands that what is happening now will soon be finished.

Our pupils will also benefit from advance warning of changes that happen throughout the school day. Each transition, from one lesson to the next, to and from break, at the start and end of each day, is a transition and a change for our pupils. We can prepare them for transitional change by giving a warning when activities are about to end. A series of warnings that the activity is going to finish in five minutes, two minutes and one minute may be helpful.

The pupil can then be given a final warning that the activity is going to end in ten, nine, eight ... These warning can, of course, be given to the whole class.

Pupils said that they find it easier when information and clear and concise instructions are **written down** or presented visually, rather than only being presented verbally. If your pupil can read, we can help by writing down the instruction or presenting the information in a structured, sequential format, in the order that they need to carry it out.

We can also support the pupils' need for predictability and routine by being consistent in our expectations. Expectations about the quantity and quality of output need to be explicit and, if possible, visualised. Specify the number of questions to be answered, the time to complete the learning task, the quantity of writing expected. Recognise that our pupils may need support to identify where to begin and 'finish' a learning task and how to organise their time to work through the task. It may be relevant to introduce a predictable, methodical and consistent approach to learning tasks, which supports the pupil's need for predictability and routine. The pupil should be aware of the quantity and quality of work expected, how they will know that they have 'finished' and what is next on the timetable. It may also be helpful for the pupil to see examples or models of a completed task so that they can visualise exactly what is expected of them.

We can also support pupils by speaking clearly and slowly and telling them exactly what they need to do. Instructions should be given in the order that they need to be carried out with key words emphasised and superfluous information kept to a minimum. We can help by asking the pupil to tell us or a peer what they need to do to check their understanding.

Unstructured times

Pupils request a quiet/safe space they could access at break-/lunchtime, preferably with fewer pupils around them and structured activities on offer. Some pupils said that they would prefer to play in a space where activities were provided by an adult, with more structure and more resources and activities available. However, other pupils found access to open spaces helpful as this gave opportunities to engage in more physical activities (which may involve less verbal interaction) and gave access to as much personal space as they needed.

Some pupils request some quiet time to re-regulate and recharge their batteries because they find social interactions tiring and stressful. We should give pupils time and space to be alone should they ask for this. While some pupils need this, others may enjoy a lunchtime club which could be offered as an alternative to the playground. This should take place in a quiet/safe place, so the pupil has time away from their classroom. An adult could support social interaction with a small group of pupils. Pupils should be able to choose to attend the club where activities and resources which they enjoy are available. Role play could also be supported. Pupils reported that, by sharing in an activity, they find it easier to engage in social interaction and the stress of unpredictable social interactions is reduced. Traditional games, which have clear rules and a repetitive structure, are also preferred. Pupils also said that they find it helpful to join clubs related to their interests. This may support social inter-actions as pupils engage with friends and peers who hold interests in common.

Other things that may help pupils manage the social and sensory experience of lunchtime are: staggering breaktimes to reduce crowding on the playground; zoning the playground so different activities take place in different spaces; offering 'quiet zones' with rugs to sit on and books to read; introducing adult-led games and activities with adults or older peers investing time in teaching children how to play these games; offering more resources for the pupils to play with; extending and increasing the type and number of lunchtime clubs on offer; displaying the Zones of Regulation visuals to support discussion about emotional regulation.

Homework/home learning

Home learning is identified as unhelpful and stressful by most pupils. It is the only part of school which was put it the house of worries by some pupils and it was never placed in the house of good things. Pupils feel that learning should be confined to school and find it difficult to accept that school could be brought into the home environment. Pupils are often exhausted by the demands of the school day and the demands of homework risk meltdown and shutdown.

Homework is a huge concern for pupils and, therefore, their families and often causes stress and arguments in families. As teachers, we should discuss with the family whether the benefits of home learning outweigh the negative impact on the pupil and the family and agree the expectations collaboratively. Written home learning rules, which are agreed with the pupil, the family and the teacher, may be helpful.

When discussing home learning with the family, consideration should be given to:

What is going to be most beneficial to the pupil, it may be reading every night and discussing the text.

Try to present the learning in a way which is acceptable to the pupil.

Offer learning tasks with a structured and consistent layout which the pupil can become familiar with.

Accept alternative means of demonstrating understanding which minimise the need for writing.

Set the expectations at the start of the week and give the pupil a week to complete the learning tasks.

Acknowledge to the pupil that you are aware that they have completed the home learning.

Pupils are able to suggest other strategies they would find helpful. These include offering an on-site homework club, providing homework rules and not giving open-ended tasks (especially in English) as homework.

Teachers' Toolbox

In the Teachers' Toolbox I suggest a number of tools and strategies which are simple, cheap and easy to implement. The emphasis, as always, is on a whole-class approach.

Initially, it may be helpful to use this checklist as a guide to reflect on your practice. This checklist is adapted from the National Autistic Society. It reflects what the pupils told us they would find helpful and is designed to help us to create autism-affirming classrooms and schools. The checklist may be helpful to teachers and pupils (Tables 6.1 and 6.2).

Table 6.1 Checklist for an autism-affirming classroom

Adaptation or adjustment	√ Doing it	√ Having a go	√ Not doing it yet
Spoken to the child to gather their views.			
Discussed pupil passport with them.			
Aware that the child is probably 'masking' their anxiety and aware that they may not be feeling ok.			
Support is given subtlety and skilfully and not just to one child.			
Instructional language is clear, explicit and in the positive (supported by a visual if possible).			
Adults adjust or reduce superfluous language (keywords only).			
Instructions are 'chunked' or broken down.			
Instructions are given in the order they will happen.			
Time given to process information, instructions and questions.			
Notice how long the child needs to process information – it may be several seconds.			
Child given pre-warning before being asked a question.			
Child's attention is gained, using their name, before an instruction is given.			
Ensure they are aware if a 'group' instruction includes them.			
Instructions are written down or printed.			
Child told explicitly what they need to do.			
Adults model appropriate language, including phrases to use with peers.			
The environment is organised and labelled (appropriate to the child's developmental level).			
Children (and adults) are clear about the structure of the day. Visual timetable on display and referred to throughout the day. visual from visual timetable as each activity is 'finished'. Advance warning is given of any changes, e.g., use of whoops or change visual.			
Variety of visual resources used to support teaching, learning and communication, e.g. now-next boards, timers, choice and motivator boards.			

(Continued)

Table 6.1 (Continued)

Adaptation or adjustment	√ Doing it	√ Having a go	√ Not doing it yet
Notice how the environmental, sensory and social is affecting the child, noise, teacher voice, temperature, seating position, etc.			
Ear defenders, sensory cushions available.			
Awareness of appropriate motivators/ use of positive praise and clear reward systems in place. Remember for younger children rewards need to be immediate.			
Preparation for transition. Transition from place-to-place or activity-to-activity is clearly signalled with visual or concrete resources to support. For example, timers, song, objects to aid transition.			
Calming activities or objects to reduce anxiety available.			
Calm/safe space available inside or/and outside the classroom.			
Own work/concentration station available.			
Variety of concrete objects used to support teaching and learning, e.g. demonstrations, models, examples.			
Consideration has been given to seating position, collaborative learning and learning partner.			
Learning steps are clear and feedback is given.			
All staff respond in a consistent way to the child.			

Table 6.2 Checklist for pupils to select any adaptations and adjustments which they would find helpful

Helpful Strategies
Child's Name:
Class:
Prepare me before the lesson by explaining what it will be about.
Offer visuals or concrete resources.
I find these visuals helpful …
Explain the learning and break it down into multiple learning steps.
Let me go to my quiet/safe place.
My preferred seating position is …
My preferred learning/talk partner is …

(Continued)

Table 6.2 (Continued)

Helpful Strategies

Use the whole-class visual timetable throughout the day.

Check that I know what I need to do next.

Use traffic lights or paper clips to check that I am feeling ok.

Offer me movement breaks.

Use short simple instructions. Give me one at a time and check that I understand. Repeat instructions in same words rather than different ones.

Write instructions down as a list so I can tick them off when completed.

Use my name before asking or giving instructions.

Give me time to think about what I need to do.

Give me time to think about what I need to say.

Explain metaphorical language and idioms.

Explain any changes to routine before they happen.

Tell me if I am going to have a different teacher.

Please let me work alone rather than in a group where possible. If in a group, give clear rules and roles in writing.

Use visual prompts on cards or photographs, or consistent non-verbal signs (sit, look, listen, hand up, wait, quiet) to tell me what I need to do.

Please don't ask me a question in front of the whole class.

Set me explicit and clear expectations e.g. how many lines to write, how many questions to answer, how long to listen.

Use a visual timer.

Put a green 'start' dot on my book and a line to show where to finish.

Get me a help card to use when I need help.

Let me use a 'concentration station'.

Let me wear ear defenders.

Help me at break and lunchtime and find a quiet space for me.

Model that making mistakes is ok and a part of the learning process.

Use incentives based on my interests which are ...

My views

Most pupils said that predictability and routine is helpful. Daily visual timetables can be used in all classrooms throughout the school and weekly timetables should be visible to the pupils. Visual timetables can be displayed vertically or horizontally (Figures 6.1 to 6.6).

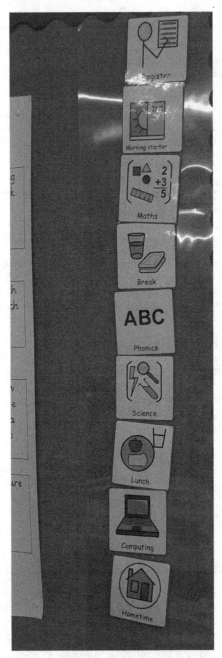

Figure 6.1 Whole-class visual timetable.

Widgit Symbols © Widgit Software Ltd 2002–2024 www.widgit.com

Figure 6.2 Whole-class visual timetable.

Widgit Symbols © Widgit Software Ltd 2002–2024 www.widgit.com

Some pupils may benefit from individual visual timetables.

Figure 6.3 An individual visual timetable.

Widgit Symbols © Widgit Software Ltd 2002–2024 www.widgit.com

Figure 6.4 An individual visual timetable.

Widgit Symbols © Widgit Software Ltd 2002–2024 www.widgit.com

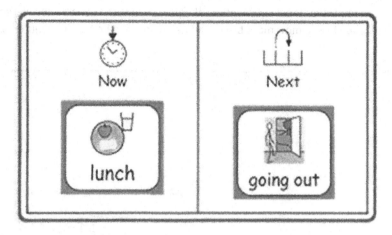

Figure 6.5 A now and next board.

Widgit Symbols © Widgit Software Ltd 2002–2024 www.widgit.com

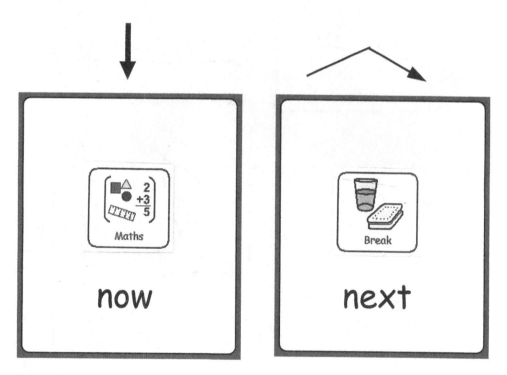

Figure 6.6 A now and next board.

Widgit Symbols © Widgit Software Ltd 2002–2024 www.widgit.com

Most pupils requested breaks throughout the day. To ensure support is delivered skilfully and subtlety, brain break, movement break and help cards can be helpful (Figures 6.7).

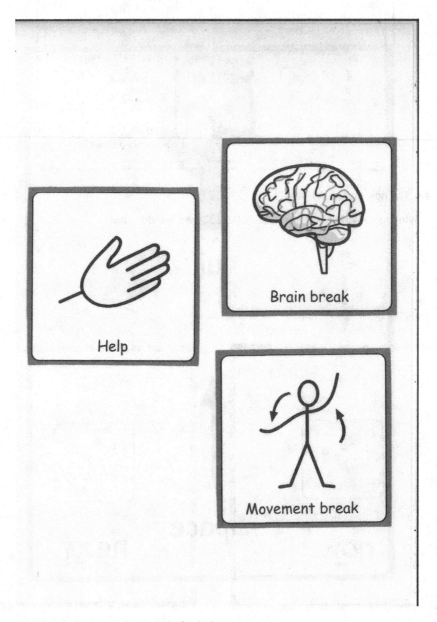

Figure 6.7 Visuals to support requests for help.

Widgit Symbols © Widgit Software Ltd 2002–2024 www.widgit.com

Pupils asked for subtle means of communication. Traffic light visuals can be used to communicate how a pupil is feeling (Figures 6.8 and 6.14).

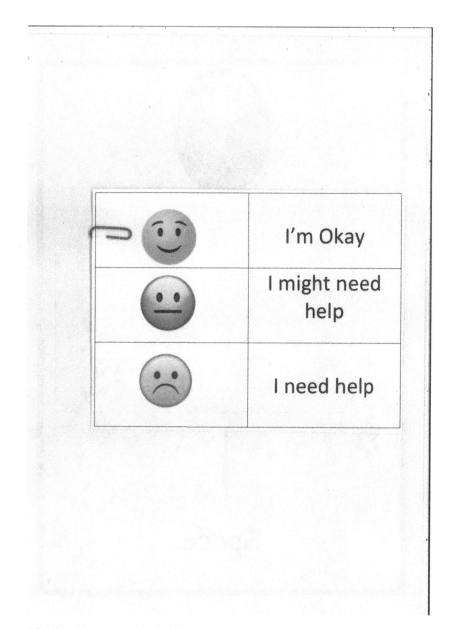

Figure 6.8 Visual to communicate that help is needed.

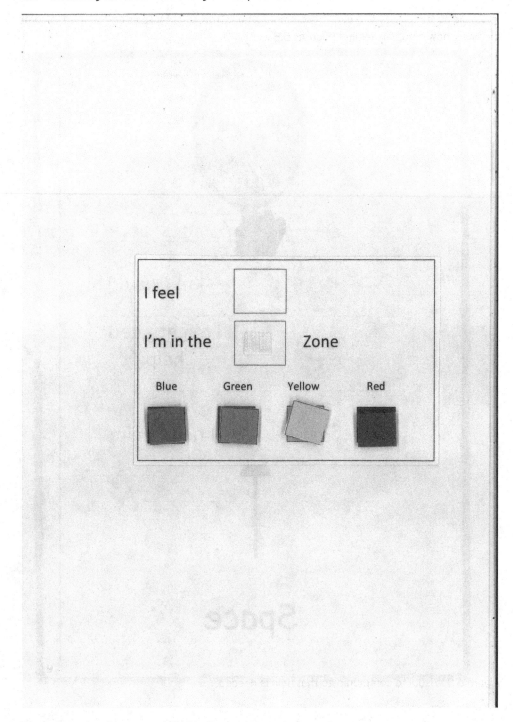

Figure 6.9 Visual to support that help may be needed.

Based on the original work, The Zones of Regulation™ Curriculum by Leah Kuypers 2011, ©Think Social Publishing, Inc. All Rights.

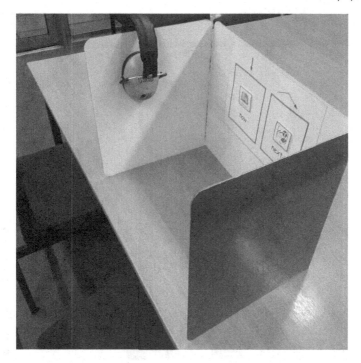

Figure 6.10 Individual 'concentration station' may support focus and attention for some pupils.

Figure 6.11 Ear defenders may help to manage the sensory environment.

Figure 6.12 Unconditional access to a quiet place was requested by most pupils.

Widgit Symbols © Widgit Software Ltd 2002–2024 www.widgit.com.

Pupils would like instructions to be written down and requested that learning tasks were broken down into small learning steps.

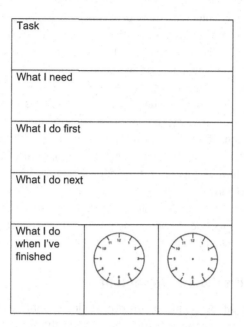

Figure 6.13 Visual task planners can support pupils starting and working through a learning task.

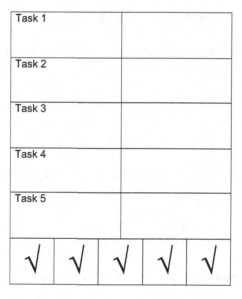

Figure 6.14 Visual task planners can support pupils starting and working through a learning task.

Pupil perspectives

The challenges which many pupils describe are remarkably consistent, namely feeling over-whelmed by the sensory environment of the classroom and the school in general; struggling as the demands of the curriculum increase, particularly in subjects with increased demands for writing; feeling that we do not understand the support that may be needed and the necessity to deliver this support skilfully and subtly; their need to 'escape' from sensory and social overload at break times and a heartfelt loathing of home learning/homework

The support which pupils request is remarkably similar across many schools, namely: the reassurance of predictability and routine and visual timetables to support this; access to quiet/safe places throughout the day; regular brain, sensory and/or movement breaks within and outside the classroom; access to a quiet/safe space at break times; support with writing and reduced demands for writing (frequency and quantity); clear instructions, written down and flexibility with homework stipulations (Connor, 2000; Dedridge, 2007; Humphrey and Lewis, 2008; Saggers, Hwang and Mercer, 2011; Parsons et al., 2011; Goodall, 2020).

Pupils request that we hide the necessary support or ensure that it is offered more widely to peers. Other adjustments, requested by the pupils, are dependent on the individual perspective of the pupil and can be gathered using the three houses approach.

The classroom and school environment

As I have already highlighted, feelings of anxiety, particularly in the classroom, are reported by our pupils. For some pupils, the sensory experience of the school; touch, noise, temperature and the confusion of the message behind a firm voice, adds to feelings of anxiety. The pupils highlight that they find being in noisy, crowded, confined spaces (the classroom) particularly difficult to manage.

If I'm in a classroom with everyone else, I find it even harder.

*

When going into class it's really noisy'cus everybody's budging past you – it's like traffic rush hour. Sometimes it bothers me and sometimes it doesn't.

*

I don't like people touching me.

*

Some people [are] hard to sit next to.

*

It's just too hot, all the time, the windows don't help.

*

Can you think when it's noisy?

*

Don't like noise or queues.

*

Have ear plugs, and ear covers [defenders] at school – they help.

*

Pinch ears to stop noise [shows me].

*

Very noisy. I can cope with a couple of noises since I can have a distraction like talking but if I can't really talk then it's painful.

*

Sometimes it's noisy. Not really [bother me] since I have to try and find a distraction. I'm very good at trying to find a distraction. There are two things. One is to draw and one is to chat secretly. Drawing takes my mind off nearly everything and chatting also does the exact same thing. I think drawing's a better option though since it's a lot more calmer. Sometimes when I talk, I get a bit fizzy, not in the excited way in the worried way.

Pupils in other schools share similar experiences of the sensory aspects of the classroom environment. They also find the noise, temperature and number of pupils in a relatively confirmed space difficult to manage. The impact of noise is the factor which is mentioned most frequently. This is followed by touch.

Open with quite a few rooms and lots of open spaces and lots of windows.

*

[My dream school] would be a big school with only a few people.

*

It would have one or two rooms for people to go to relax … calm down when they need it.

*

Places to de-stress outside if needed.

*

Lots of space around the school.

*

Individual workstations designed by pupils.

Saggers et al. report (2011, p. 184):

I think it would have to be – you know some children in class like to make a lot of noise and racket and they're just a bit too noisy and stuff like that. I reckon those type of students that try and stand out; those are the hardest thing here.

*

I don't like it when there's, you know, the rooms are – when they're cramped, well just small.

Goodall added (2020, p. 87):

I was stressed trying to cope with the noise, the large class sizes, the constantly changing people.

*

There was too much noise and too many people to deal with.

*

I felt closed in and like I couldn't breathe as there were so many people.

*

It was so difficult being in there all day.

Goodall also reported (2020, p. 88):

> Too crowded, too noisy, the classrooms were too noisy. There was too much noise making me more stressed.
>
> *
>
> It was too overwhelming and every single day was really noisy. It is too crowded.
>
> *
>
> The noise and business. It was a new piece of pressure each time going in [to lunch]. I went through whole days without eating to avoid it.

When Connor (2020) asked pupils what helps them to learn best, most children chose working in a small group.

Learning and the curriculum

Pupils describe how their anxiety is heightened in the classroom as the pressure of work (amount and difficulty) increases through the week and as they move through the school. Pupils are able to identify preferred and less favoured subjects and lessons. Practical and factual subjects with reduced demands for writing are generally preferred by the pupils.

> Makes me feel bad. The noise, the pressure of doing the work.
>
> *
>
> Well, the teachers didn't really understand, and they gave us too much pressure and too much work to do and they gave us work after work after work. I think most years.
>
> *
>
> They gave you really pressure and I didn't really care about it but they made you really care about it.
>
> *
>
> I don't like pressure [of the curriculum] on me.

Many pupils place English in their house of worries:

> Don't like English, I think it's the writing.
>
> *
>
> Lessons that aren't going well, umm, yes. I think English isn't going well. Writing, writing, writing, I'm pretty good at reading. Also spelling, that's NOT going well at all I'm really bad at spelling. Yer, it's very hard.
>
> *
>
> I write very fast and don't think of my ideas. I can't really write very descriptive language. I make lots of mistakes.
>
> *
>
> I also find checking my English very, very tricky. There was only one time I was on fire editing seven paragraphs.
>
> *
>
> I don't like English. I think it's just the writing.
>
> *

I want to stop doing English.

*

My hand gets sore. I hold my pen too hard.

*

My favourite subjects are:
Number 1 social learning
Number 2 PE
Number 3 Topic
Number 4 Music
Number 5 English – writing.

Generally, pupils find mathematics more enjoyable than English but this is not exclusively the case.

I really like maths,'cus, it's not like a lot of writing and it's more like you have to think.

*

Maths is going well, yeah I'm good at maths.

*

I can finish all my maths in the lesson.

*

Maths, and it's still my favourite. Um, I think because it's a wrong and a right answer and it's not you have to do this to find, to find out this.

*

In English I've not written as much but in maths I'm the same [as my friends].

Pupils express that they enjoy other subjects. These tend to be creative, physical or fact-based.

Art was good. I liked getting the art award.

*

I'd like to have more time to do D.T.

*

I like fun lessons.

*

Sometimes I like science, PE and music.

*

I like learning about facts.

*

I just love PE so much, I don't like running two laps around, I like indoor rounders.

*

Science is my favourite. I am so good at science.

*

Art ... it's not going well but it's going well. Music, I guess is going well, music. I do drums, yes. It's going well, I love drums but it's not really a lesson.

*

I like music because I sing songs. I'm good at singing.

Pupils in other schools also find the demands and pace of the curriculum increasingly difficult to manage and highlight that they find subjects which demand extended pieces of writing particularly challenging.

Saggers et al. reported (2011, pp. 179, 180):

> Sometimes it's a bit crazy how we all have to hand in all the assignments in at once.
>
> *
>
> I don't really like English all that much. It's too much work ... too much writing, and too much assignments ...
>
> *
>
> Maybe the stress of knowing that this is what is going to help me get into the workforce, that's about it.
>
> *
>
> Things get too overwhelming with work and stuff.
>
> *
>
> Probably just how much there is. Yeah, it eventually gets ... exhausting.
>
> *
>
> If I had a computer, it would be better. Because I'm faster on the computer than I am at writing, and some people can't read my writing.

Goodall further stated (2020, p. 88):

> This is me pulling my hair out as I am so stressed at teachers, the work.

Teachers – understanding of the support which is needed and how to deliver it

Our understanding of the adaptations and adjustments needed, and how these are offered and delivered, impacts negatively and positively on our pupils' experience of school. As I have already highlighted, the pupils recognise that we have the biggest single impact on their experience of school and understand that we are in control of the adaptations and adjustments which they need.

Pupils often feel too embarrassed to use the adaptations and adjustments which are in place to support them and prefer to hide their need for help and support from us, rather than expose their need for it. Pupils are working hard to hide the fact that they need help and support and this leads to unnecessary feelings of stress and anxiety.

> Do you think the teachers notice when you're feeling stressed or do you hide it from them?
>
> *
>
> No, I probably hide it.
>
> *
>
> I come in [to the classroom] and I don't know what to do.
>
> *

Usually the teachers would use it for the whole class even if it might be only like a group of people who needed it. Then they don't know who needs it and who doesn't need it. I'd be ok with that.

*

What about when you are asked a question in class?

*

Well, I don't really like it because sometimes she will choose me when I don't have my hand up.

*

Would it be ok if she chose you when you had your hand up?

*

Yeh, I'm ok with that but some teachers have no hands up.

*

I'd rather do it in a small room, but I'd rather have a few other people.

*

Wanting teachers to understand I need support - with work and getting in the right frame of mind.

*

And I think sometimes he [the teacher] might say, I'm not going to choose you [to answer a question].

*

Would you like someone with you in the classroom or would you rather go out to a group room?

*

I think I'd like someone in the classroom so it's not just me. Usually in English and maybe one other lesson.

*

Somethings it's the whole class and I don't know [if the teacher is talking to me].

Pupils report that written (rather than verbal) instructions are helpful.

If it's a subject I like and am good at I can [understand the instruction].

*

Easier if it's the instructions are written.

*

I could have my own [copy], written down.

*

I wish I did know but I don't. Sometimes I make a little plan [written down] and people kinda make fun of me. I just do a very small plan. I do all the steps because it kinda gets my mind to action. And everyone said that's a very small plan. It helped quite a lot because when I look at the board it's up there and I can't adjust and if it's up there and I'm writing down here I kinda forget to look at it. If I had it down there, I'd do that, look there, and my brains already in action.

*

Yer and sometimes I have a notebook with it written in so I don't need to keep looking at the board.

*

Would it be helpful to have instructions written on the board?

*

Yes, sometimes she does that but sometimes I don't know that she's written it down. So sometimes I don't look on the board in the morning, so I don't know that there are any instructions. I don't want to say it in front of the whole class.

*

Does your teacher know that it would be helpful to have the instructions written on the board every morning?

*

No, but it would.

Pupils said that visual timetables are helpful.

If there's a change, they tell me or I can look at the timetable. So instead of going to English you're going to a different lesson they'd probably tell us but if they didn't know they wouldn't tell us.

*

We have our timetables on the wall so I can come in and look at it. I like that.

*

I like the [visual] timetable because sometimes the teachers might change around what we're doing.

*

Well once, I was having a really good day and it said maths at the end of the day which I like so I was really excited, and she went to talk to the other teachers, and they changed it to English. Well, I didn't really like it, at all.

*

I think I have a good idea. If I could have a change [symbol] so that I could write on it. And then I could have one at school and Ms S could write on it if we're changing something tomorrow. And one at home so I know.

*

On the timetable sometimes she will say that we're doing this, but she won't actually change it on the timetable. Just tell us that we're doing this different. And sometimes she might not and when it comes to the time that we are going to do maths she'll say change of plan; we're going to do English. AH!

*

[I like it] when we have the same lessons each week for the whole year.

Pupils request breaks and access to safe/quiet places.

Do you ever think that you'd like to leave the classroom for a brain break?
Yes.
How often do you think that you'd like to leave the classroom?

Usually Wednesdays and Fridays, and sometimes on Thursdays'cus most of those
days there's lots of the writing, there's lots of English on Wednesday and Friday
and then there's lots of writing on Thursday. Then we have PE which I like.
Do you leave the classroom for a brain break on Wednesday, Friday and Thursday?'
I'd like to say, can I get something.

*

Would you like to go and sit outside the classroom for 5 minutes?
I'd like to do it, but I'd like to say can I get something from my bag, instead of giv-
ing her something.
Would that help you?
Yes.
How long would you need to be outside the classroom?
I think two to three minutes would be enough.

*

Brain break - only used it once. When I was crying. It would have helped me more.

*

If I'm in a classroom with everyone else, I find it even harder [to ask for a brain
break].
When you're in lessons can you come out if you need a break?
Yes, If I'm feeling stressful about anything, I can come out'
How often do you do that?
Not very much. 'Cus it's a bit embarrassing going out so I just sit down.

*

I'd like to go out into the corridor for a break.

*

Movement breaks are helpful. Why can't everyone have them?

*

Well, I'd maybe have about half an hour one day after each other or one day skip
a day to have half an hour out of lessons just to take a break. Just so we can slow
down because the work does get really fast. Or even half an hour break most days.

Pupils are aware of other adaptations and adjustments which would be helpful.

[I'd] like to choose who I can sit next to.

*

I'd rather just have the work and be able to get on with it.

*

When we've finished a lesson, I'm like ok hand out the maths books. This is how I
know the lesson is finished.

*

All those phrases are weird. Right now I'm going to go and hit the road. Well drive
safe. No, literally, I'm going to go and hit the road. Why would a teacher say that?
I could be in a smaller class, [with fewer pupils].

*

Usually, I like to sit next to boys because I can get most lessons done. And when they say talk to each other I think that it's easier for boys to communicate with each other.

*

Um, I just ask the teacher that I'm confused.

*

Had enough support from the lovely Mrs. F.

*

English is ok because I'm told what I need to write for each bit.

*

I can ask the teacher for help.

Misunderstanding of the support needed and the necessity for the subtle and skilful delivery of this support was a common source of anxiety amongst pupils in many schools.
 Goodall reported (2020, pp. 104, 107, 96, respectively):

Recognise my difficulties but don't single them out.

*

If they laid the work out step by step ... I can follow written down, but not just verbally.

*

I couldn't approach them [teachers] due to my anxiety.

Saggers, Hwang and Mercer added (2011, p. 181):

I sort of feel a bit well, just different, when I'm just the one getting help.

*

I just don't like it when I get, sort of like, treated differently.

*

I just don't like them making it so obvious.

Humphrey and Lewis also reported (2008, p. 38):

I don't like people coming to my lessons.

*

If they were following me then the other students know that there's something different about me and I don't like it at all.

*

I don't really like the extra attention.

*

That's the worst thing ever [some support in some subjects].

Saggers, Hwang and Mercer fed back (2011, p. 180):

Like in math class because I'm really good at math, I'll tell the teacher that if I need help. I'll ask them for the help, because if I don't, don't worry. Because I listen to music to help me with math ... Music sort of calms me down ...it helps me concentrate a bit better on what I'm doing.

Dedridge added (2007, p. 14):

> I find that teachers talk too much ... talking and talking ... and I lose some of the stuff they said at the start. Sometimes they tell you to copy something and they carry on talking to you and you don't know whether to listen or write. If you get something wrong, it stops you writing but they keep talking and talking. Sometimes when I ask, they just come out with a channel of words. Then when they have finished, they say 'Do you understand now?' So I nod because I am afraid, they will just keep talking.
>
> *
>
> I wish teachers would make it clearer what they want me to do. If they made it clearer, I wouldn't mess it up and I would do it right. Most teachers don't make it clear enough. The worksheets are sometimes hard to understand. They should make them clearer.

Dedridge further stated (2007, p. 19):

> My helper writes down a list of what I've got to do in the lesson and I tick it off as I do it. This really helps. My old helper used to talk to me all the time. She was talking in one ear and the teacher was talking in the other ear.
>
> *
>
> I forget things very easily. My brain is like that cheese that has holes in it. My teacher told me to write lists to help me remember. It really helps me.

Saggers, Hwang and Mercer also contributed (2011, p. 181):

> Just if I didn't have it, [additional support] I'd probably be in much worse condition.
>
> *
>
> I think I'm pretty fond of [my support teacher] It's for me, it helps me, so yeah, I'm fine with it.
>
> *
>
> Well, I sort of feel a bit well, just different, when I get, when I'm just the one getting help ... No, but I just don't like it when I get, sort of like, treated differently.
>
> *
>
> Sort of, I just don't like them making it so obvious.
>
> *
>
> Sometimes I guess, but I don't like it sometimes. Actually most of the time. I don't like teachers sitting next to me.
>
> *
>
> What if they're helping everybody in the class, not just you is that okay?
>
> *
>
> That makes me feel better.

Goodall also added (2020, p. 109):

> It would be nice to have little areas of the classroom to escape to if stressed.
>
> *

Yes, it [a quiet/safe place] would be nice.

*

I would like my own safe space. Knowing it was there would have helped.

*

Comfortable places to hide in the classroom with headphones if stressed.

*

Sometimes I just went to the toilet to sit and breathe … and get away from the noise and pressure.

*

I would like more frequent breaks even if short … this would make me happy.

Unstructured times

There are a number of things that the pupils find challenging about break time and lunch time. However, some pupils are able to identify adaptations and adjustments which they find helpful.

Breaktime and lunchtime

I don't like going outside at break, it's boring.

*

I quite like it [lunchtime club] 'cus usually in the hall it gets noisy and it usually gets hot.

*

I like being able to draw at break and lunch, somewhere quiet.

*

I'd like to pick a person and one break each week stay in class and draw.

*

Lunchtime club is good.

*

I like the field.

*

I liked playing with children in there. They were younger than me.

*

I really like it there because there are things to do.

*

The field is boring – only green and grass.

*

In the playground sometimes we play basketball.

*

There's quite a lot of things to do at break and lunchtime. Play football and basket-ball I guess, have a little chat, play in the sun. Loads of different things.

*

The playground is scary.

The sensory environment of the lunch hall is challenging for some pupils, while it did not bother others.

> The assembly hall was the same as the lunch hall and that's disgusting, and you had to sit on the floor and that's disgusting.
>
> *
>
> I don't want to go into the hall [to eat lunch].
>
> *
>
> Too loud in the dinner hall.
>
> *
>
> I'd like people to be quieter in the dinner hall.
>
> *
>
> Queue in the dinner hall – I hate queues.
>
> *
>
> I like eating in the hall.
>
> *
>
> Never think that it's too noisy.

While pupils are mainly positive about break time and lunch time, and talk about playing with their friends, many secondary school pupils describe spending time alone and finding places in the school which they can escape to.

> OK, if I talk to some friends.
>
> *
>
> I just got ready for the next lesson, or I do my homework, or go and say hello to the teacher. ·
>
> *
>
> It's usually OK – I go to the special needs building and do my homework at break and lunchtime.
>
> *
>
> I prefer to stay inside and go to a club. ·
>
> *
>
> I spend the time in the homework club. ·
>
> *
>
> I find the lunchtimes hard. ·
>
> *
>
> I don't really play with anyone or play games or anything: when I'm doing nothing, lunchtime seems a long time. ·
>
> *
>
> It's worse than in class because in class you are busy—I try to stay away from other people. ·
>
> *
>
> I spend most time in the music room, or I keep occupied and away from the playground as far as possible. ·
>
> *
>
> I don't do much; I stand around or go to the library.

Home learning/homework

The pupils express strongly held views on home learning/homework and most pupils placed it in their house of worries. Some pupils express positive views about everything in the school, except homework. Pupils find open-ended tasks with increased demands for writing particularly challenging. Pupils are able to identify adaptations and adjustments which alleviate some of the anxiety around homework.

It causes arguments [at home].

*

It's wasting all day.

*

I don't like homework.

*

Sometimes I get worried – I forget to do the homework.

*

Sometimes I forgot to write homework in my journal but usually I did remember.

*

Sometimes if you have something to do at home you can't do the homework.

*

Good thing to not have any homework.

*

My dream is not doing homework. Just do fun activities.

*

I hate homework.

*

I don't like homework because it's too long, too long for me to do it … for about 10 minutes … 10 minutes is too long.

*

But when you get home, you're supposed to relax, not do more work. That's my opinion. I only get 3 hours to relax. You might thing that's plenty but when you see the weekend you see loads and they go really quickly and 3 hours turns into 30 minutes.

*

Rather I didn't get it – I don't think anybody likes homework!

*

In Australia it's so good, you don't get homework.

*

I needed someone to help me. My mum or my dad. They hate homework too.

*

I said I don't like having homework!

Many pupils found English homework particularly challenging.

Oh English, English was the worst.

*

I'm like nnnooo, not one of those ones that you have to write a lot.

*

It's fine a bit of homework, maybe as a little revision but not comprehension, that takes an hour, reading for 20 minutes, that's fine.

*

In the comprehension I think it would be easier if like there was a sheet and you just wrote down on the sheet, so you'd circle the ones that you thought were correct. And there are questions and you can just answer them on the other side and you just stick it in instead of writing all of the other things out.

*

Maths is ok, comprehension which I'd like to change.

*

The worst homework is English.

*

Actually, I quite like grammar. 'Cus it's one of those ones where you have to think and it's not one of those ones that you have to write a lot. Like in maths you usually just write the answer.

The pressure to complete home learning everyday results in anxiety building through the week:

They kept on giving you homework everyday. Give you homework one day after another after another.

Pupils felt it would be easier:

If they did one day, then one space, then one day.

*

Yes, that's good, that's good. Yep, perfect. Not homework every day. That's kinda bonkers.

However, pupils, who have specifically adapted homework, are more positive.

I like homework. I get one sheet of homework per week to do at the weekend.

*

I get homework on Friday to do at the weekend.

*

Homework should be harder.

*

Like homework, good homework, never get bad homework. Sometimes they [my parents] can be a little bit pushy, I don't like that. I'm glad my parents aren't pushy like the pushy uncle on Child Genius.

*

I get it done. Mum helps me – she thinks it's good.

*

Maths is good in the homework.

*

Spellings, sometimes, I think spellings is alright. I find it easier because they changed it from Monday to the other Monday, so you do Monday, Tuesday, Wednesday, Thursday, Friday and then the weekend.

*

Sometimes it was fine – when we had to measure biscuits in Year 5.

*

I like making things – no other homework.

Pupils also speak of homework rules being helpful.

It makes it easier because we have already agreed.

*

Homework rules help me.

*

If it's not in the rules, I don't do it.

*

Yes, the rules helped. I think so.

*

Once when I went home, and I did three comprehensions but apparently, I had to do a different three. They weren't in the rules, so I didn't do them.

*

I had homework rules, what I do when I get home. Yes, that was helpful.

*

J has homework rules now. If it's not on the list, then he's not doing it!

Pupils feel that if they must do homework, it is better to do it in school.

Be better to do homework at school.

*

Yes, it's very good. Me and J go there.

*

In school, in school, because when you get home you can relax, easy. And I've got some very important video games to do.

*

Easier to concentrate at school.

*

The support in class to do homework so then I know what to do.

*

It's easier when it's given on Friday 'cus I have homework club [on Friday] pupils in other schools were aligned with our pupils on their profound dislike of homework.

*

I don't like homework.

*

There's a lot more homework and assignments which I think is terrible.

*

You'll probably get this from most students, but homework [is the worst].

Saggers, Hwang and Mercer noted (2011, p. 180):

It would be [homework] assignments, I think. Getting them done I think.

Goodall revealed (2020, p. 108):

It [homework] was like a snowball going down a hill ... as you go downhill further the work build up further and further.

*

I hated the homework. I couldn't remember the homework.

Reflection

Which of the factors discussed in this chapter are having the greatest impact on your pupils?

Have you discussed each of the factors with your pupils and asked them what they would find helpful? Do pupils feel comfortable asking for the adaptations and adjustments which they need?

Are you aware of the anxiety that changing or altering these factors has on your pupils?

Have you noticed whether any of your pupils are disappearing to the toilets for extended periods?

How can you deliver support to your pupils in a way that is acceptable to them? This may mean keeping it hidden from their friends and peers.

Consider the adaptations and adjustments which should be non-negotiable as part of a whole-school approach.

How can you use pupil voice to ensure that everyone is onboard which the whole-school approach?

Summary

The third theme which emerged from conversations with our pupils was hide support for me - or I won't use it. This theme has five sub-themes: the classroom environment; learning and the curriculum; teachers; unstructured times; and homework.

Despite our best endeavours, as teachers, pupils are very firm in their belief that we do not always understand the anxiety that they are experiencing at school, and a lack of support or clumsily delivered support can add to their stress. Rejecting the help, which is needed, because it is delivered in a way that is unacceptable to the pupils, is likely to heighten these feelings.

Pupils understand that it is us, as teachers, who have the single biggest impact on their experience of school. Each of the five sub-themes is discussed in details and the adaptations and adjustments which the pupils requested are highlighted. The changes to practice which the pupils requested may lead to a more positive school experience and may go some way to alleviate feelings of stress and anxiety, which our pupils are often working hard to hide. I suggest that many of the adaptations and adjustments could be part of a whole-school approach and that a whole-school approach to creating an autism-affirming school would usually be beneficial to all pupils in the school.

In the Teachers' Toolbox I suggest a number of tools and strategies which are simple, cheap and easy to implement. The emphasis, as always, is on a whole-class approach. The chapter closes with the pupils' views, thoughts and feelings on the theme.

In this chapter, I have outlined:

Discussion on the theme Hide support for me– or I won't use it.

Discussion on the sub-themes: classroom environment; learning and the curriculum; teachers; unstructured times; and homework.

An explanation of how to use the pupils' perspectives to support us in generating a greater understanding of the support which our pupils request and how to deliver this support skilfully and subtly.

Pupils' perspectives on the theme and sub-themes.

References

Bogdashina, O. (2011). Sensory perceptual issues in autism: Why we should listen to those who experience them. Annales Universitatis Paedagogicae Cracoviensis. *Studia Psychologica* 1: 145–160. www.ceeol.com/search/article-detail?id=42167

Connor, M. (2000). Asperger syndrome (autistic spectrum disorder) and the self-reports of comprehensive school students. *Educational Psychology in Practice*, *16*(3), 285–296.

Dedridge, S. (2007). Including pupils with autistic spectrum disorder. In R. Macconville, S. Dedridge and A. Gyulai. *Looking at Inclusion: Listening to the Voices of Young People*. (pp. 15–38). Sage Publications Ltd.

Goodall, C. (2020). *Understanding the Voices and Educational Experiences of Autistic Young People: From Research to Practice*. Routledge.

Gross, J. (2015). *Beating Bureaucracy in Special Educational Needs: Helping SENCOs Create a Work Life Balance*. Routledge.

Humphrey, N. and Lewis, S. (2008). Make me normal: The views and experiences of pupils on the autistic spectrum in mainstream secondary schools. *Autism*, *12*(1), 23–46.

National Autistic Society. (2023). National Autistic Society Education Report, www.autism.org.uk/what-we-do/news/education-report-2023

Parsons, S., Guldberg, K., MacLeod, A., Jones, G., Prunty, A. and Balfe, T. (2011). International review of the evidence on best practice in educational provision for children on the autism spectrum. *European Journal of Special Needs Education*, *26*(1), 47–63, DOI: 10.1080/08856257.2011.543532

Saggers, B., Hwang, Y. and Mercer, L. (2011). Your voice counts: Listening to the voice of high school students with autism spectrum disorder. *Australasian Journal of Special Education*, *35*(2), 173–190. www.cambridge.org/core/terms

Chapter seven

Concluding thoughts and reflections on what an autism-affirming school should be like

Chapter outline

In this chapter, I draw some conclusions on how we may begin to create autism-affirming schools, from our pupils' perspectives. I stress that all the adaptations and adjustments discussed in this book were requested by the pupils themselves and may, therefore, give us a unique perspective into what autism-affirming schools should be like. I share personal reflections and leave the last word to four of our pupils whose views, thoughts and feelings on their experience of school were the catalyst for this book.

Conclusion

Autism is increasingly being considered more positively as a shared culture; a way of understanding and communicating which may be shared with other autistic people. The way autism is described, experienced, identified and diagnosed is impacted increasingly by self-advocacy and the evolving perspectives of autism as we shift away from a medical-deficit model to a strength-based, identity-first approach.

Human rights legislation reminds us that everyone has the right to be heard and citizenship is dependent on active and meaningful participation in our lives, including being involved in decisions which affect us. However, I question whether anything much has changed for many autistic children and young people.

Historically, autistic children and young people have not been meaningfully involved in decisions which affect them and have not been enabled to share their valuable insights of their unique, lived experiences. The historic failings in seeking the voices of autistic children and young people have impacted negatively on many autistic children and young people as they have been excluded from decisions which impact their lives. Personal perspectives and autographical reflections of autistic adults on their school experiences serve as powerful testimonies and remind us that the negative consequences of not being listened to remain long into adulthood.

As autism prevalence rates continue to rise, an increasing number of children and young people may be, unintentionally, let down by schools, and other sectors.

The experiences and outcomes for autistic children and young people continue to be poor across multiple sectors, including education. Too often, autistic children and young people

DOI: 10.4324/9781003396499-7

are not able to fulfil their potential and, despite best endeavours, schools and other providers are often ill-equipped to understand the support which the children and young people need. Inconsistent practice makes this worse. This has resulted in poor academic outcomes, high levels of absenteeism and exclusion, high university dropout rates, low rates of employment and poor health outcomes.

Throughout the book, I have stressed that listening to our pupils' personal accounts of school is important if we are to improve outcomes for our children and young people. Using pupil voice as an easily accessible, freely available resource, to enable more pupil advocacy and generate an understanding of how to develop strength-based, autism-affirming schools, will become increasingly important as schools continue to feel the effect of tightened school budgets. The pupils should be enabled to be advocates and given the opportunity to communicate their lived experiences of the school. Their powerful testimonies can serve as a highly effective catalyst in generating an understanding of the adjustments and adaptations which have been requested by the pupils themselves.

I describe a tool which has been used to enable our pupils to express their views, thoughts and feelings of school. The three houses approach may facilitate the meaningful engagement and participation of autistic pupils. It can also be used to discover the topics, things about the school, which are important to the pupils themselves and to gather their views, thoughts and feelings on each of these topics. I have shown how the approach has been effective in uncovering the pupils' perspectives, on what was going well, what was not going well and what we need to change in school.

Previous studies, which have sought to capture pupil voice (and there are few of them), may have missed the opportunity to support the pupils in generating topics which are important to the pupils. The topics which the pupils raised may, therefore, be different to those considered previously.

Following analysis of the data, three key themes emerged: 'Understand me – I may surprise you'; 'Help me to understand – understand myself and understand others'; and 'Hide support for me – or I won't use it'. Each of these overarching themes has a number of sub-themes.

The theme 'Understand me – I may surprise you' has three sub-themes: teachers; hidden anxiety; friends and peers. Pupils requested that non-autistic people worked harder to understand their autistic world, specifically the anxiety which they were often working hard to hide.

The theme 'Help me to understand – understand myself and understand others' has two sub-themes: pupils requested support to understand themselves as autistic children; and young people and support to understand more about the non-autistic world.

The third theme 'Hide support for me – or I won't use it' has five sub-themes: the classroom environment; learning and the curriculum; teachers; unstructured times; and home learning.

Pupils felt very strongly that teachers, friends and peers should have an insightful and meaningful understanding of autism in general, and of them as autistic individuals specifically, and described how this understanding (or lack of it) had the greatest impact on their experience of school. The hope that teachers may improve their understanding of autism was universally held by pupils.

Pupils requested insight on 'both sides' (Milton, 2012). They requested a greater level of understanding from non-autistic people and requested that they were supported in developing an understanding of the non-autistic world. Adaptations and adjustments should be expected on 'both sides' and non-autistic individuals should alter their behaviour and practice accordingly. In other words, we should not be expecting autistic pupils to make all the running but should be meeting somewhere in the middle, by making the chances to our practice which the pupils themselves have requested. If our autistic pupils are not thriving in school, we should not consider this as a deficit held within the pupil but should think about the adjustments and adaptations which we need to make to enable them to have a positive school experience.

As we generate a greater understanding of autism generally and of our autistic pupils specifically, we may recognise that our pupils need support. Pupils themselves requested support but it was often rejected if they felt that it was delivered in a way that was unhelpful to them. I stressed that we may be incorrect in believing that if a pupil rejects support, it is because the support is not needed.

Our pupils may have become so adept at hiding or masking their autism that we may believe that they are coping in school when they are not. This is not a passive response for many pupils. The pupils are anxious about not being able to cope, and worried that their inability to cope may be discovered. If we fail to understand that autism comes with heightened levels of anxiety and that pupils work hard to hide this anxiety, the long-term impact on pupils can be detrimental.

A child or young person's outcomes may differ significantly depending on the inclusive culture of the setting, the understanding of the child or young person, the understanding, knowledge and expertise of the staff, the social and sensory environment, the curriculum and its delivery. Adaptations and adjustments, therefore, need to take account of each of these factors.

I advocate adopting an autism-affirming, whole-school approach which enables autistic and non-autistic pupils to be supported through a whole-school understanding, where appreciation of diversity is the norm. This means actively supporting and promoting autism and expecting everyone to make the adjustments and adaptations that are necessary so that every pupil is enabled to have a positive school experience. Adjusting practice across the school, in response to pupil voice, will benefit autistic pupils but may also be beneficial to non-autistic pupils; it will certainly not be detrimental to them.

Although I would always advocate that teachers gather the perspectives of school from their own pupils, the consistency of the narratives of a large number of autistic pupils may give us, as teachers, the confidence to understand the adaptations and adjustments which have been requested by many pupils. The consistency of the pupils' narrative is impressive and may be surprising to some. Many pupils, from several different schools, requested a greater level of understanding of autism in general, and of themselves as autistic pupils specifically, and asked for the same or similar adaptations and adjustments over and over again.

I have included quotes from many pupils from several schools, so that their views, thoughts and feelings are recorded verbatim and not paraphrased through an adult. Their narrative serves as a powerful testimony to how they often experience a lack of understanding of themselves as autistic pupils and explains why the implication of the teachers' toolbox may be helpful when working towards creating autism-affirming schools.

One of the things that is different about this book is that it is entirely underpinned by pupil voice. Listening to the voices of autistic children and young people is absolutely critical if we are to create autism-affirming schools from the pupils' perspectives. We must start to listen!

Personal reflection

In 2018, one of our autistic pupils, exhausted and dysregulated, declared that our school was 100% NOT 'autistic-friendly'. He was right to be frustrated. He was working hard to understand and function in a non-autistic school environment which he was adapting to, five days a week, 39 weeks a year.

His frustration was fundamentally an attempt to communicate his request for an enhanced understanding from non-autistic people, principally that his teachers, friends and peers increase their understanding of the autistic world and recognise and acknowledge the part that they play in the challenges which he experiences.

As self-advocacy is growing within the autistic community there is an increasing narrative that non-autistic individuals often lack insight into and understanding of the autistic world. Our autistic pupils agree whole-heartedly that not enough value is placed on teachers and the wider community understanding their autistic world.

Our pupil's declaration was a catalyst for change in our primary school, as we endeavoured to discover the views, thoughts and feelings of our autistic pupils to understand how they were experiencing the school. I listened to their voices, and the pupils became advocates for themselves and each other. The accounts of their lived experiences of the school started to generate an understanding of the changes to practice which we, as teachers, needed to make. The teachers may have been the enablers in this process, but it is the pupils who were the catalysts for change.

For our pupils, being part of an autism-affirming school, which they helped to create, is more than teachers making adjustments and adaptations to meet their needs. For a school to be truly autism-affirming, it needs to generate a meaningful sense of belonging where all pupils are celebrated as unique individuals, where a culture of diversity being the norm is supported and celebrated and that non-autistic pupils and teachers are continually thinking about what they can do to meet their autistic friends and pupils 'halfway'. This may have implications for how primary schools can, and should, change to support autistic pupils.

We have come a long way on our journey to understand what an autism-affirming school should be like from the pupils' perspective and have implemented many changes. We have found that the adaptations and adjustments we have made have often been beneficial to all pupils in the school. Anything that we have done, any changes to practice which we have implemented, have been requested by the pupils themselves.

A final word from our pupils

When 'Will' burst into the staff room of a large three-form entry primary school in 2018, he had no idea what he was about to unleash. When I caught up with his parents in 2023, his father told me that 'Will' could not remember making the declaration. Yet his statement that 'This school is 100% NOT autistic-friendly' led to many hours of reflective soul-searching and ultimately significant changes to the practice in our school.

It is some time now since I started to gather the views, thoughts and feelings of pupils on their experience of school. The pupils were instrumental in driving change, and I am grateful to the pupils for sharing their perspectives. I have kept in touch with some of the pupils from the initial cohort. It is appropriate that the final reflection is theirs.

Jack, Toby, 'Will' and Eleanor were part of the first group who were kind enough to share their views on school with me. I caught up with them six years after I first started to gather their views. They were kind enough to share their reflections on their time at primary school, consider the one thing that would have made the biggest difference to them and update me on what they are doing now. Many thanks to their parents and carers for enabling these interactions.

In line with the narrative throughout the book, the pupils discussed the level of understanding (of them as autistic pupils) amongst teachers, with Jack eloquently describing that the teachers understanding what he needed was the factor which had the most significant positive impact on him.

Jack felt that having autistic friends was a supportive factor and Toby, 'Will' and Eleanor have formed friendships initiated by interests held in common; sport, cooking and gaming.

The preferred secondary school subjects tended to be practical, or fact based: cooking, design and technology, forest school, PE, maths, science, music and history. No one named English as their preferred subject!

Toby and Jack reflected that working in groups or classes with fewer pupils was helpful and Toby remembered his preferred seating position and the positive impact of this. The pupils discussed having time to 'chill' after school, spending time outside, cooking and baking, playing sport and keeping active all helped them. They felt that having more clubs at school would have been supportive, specifically around their interests. This may have given them time to 'chill' at school away from the hustle and bustle of the playground, provided structure at difficult parts of the day and may also have supported friendships by encouraging the sharing of interests held in common. These insights suggest that the pupils have generated an understanding of themselves, are attuned with their self-regulation and understand what they need to do to support themselves.

The pupils reflected on the support that was in place. None of them mentioned teaching assistants who may have supported them. However, they felt that smaller group sessions and support with English and handwriting had been helpful. Interestingly, although homework was a worry for most of the pupils when they were in primary school, none of the pupils mentioned it in their reflections.

Jack

Jack shared that the one thing that transformed things for him at primary school was 'Having choices made the biggest differences to me. People [teachers] understood that I needed to choose an activity based on how I felt, not what they said I had to do.'

Having relocated to Yorkshire, Jack now attends a specialist secondary school with small class sizes. He is thriving both personally and academically.

> As well as maths and English, we do things like cooking, design technology, and forest school. My friends there are just like me. I try hard to be a good example in my behaviour. I love having some independence, walking my dog, and having time to chill after school.

Toby

Toby thought that primary school felt as if:

> It was a long time ago but I do remember enjoying going out to be part of smaller group sessions to help me with my learning. I also remember a moment when I

was moved to the front of the class, and that this was helpful, as being in the middle or at the back was very distracting. My Year Two teacher supported my handwriting with additional work that I had to complete and I had to do the Lexia [literacy intervention] programme, which took up lots of time, but I think it really helped my English language.

Toby is now doing well in a mainstream, local secondary school. Although he finds a number of subjects challenging, he is a hard worker and is a popular, confident, polite and kind member of his school community (and outside of it too!). His handwriting is still a struggle, and he sometimes types on a laptop at school.

These are Toby's words:

I am now in Year Nine of secondary school, where I am really happy. I am playing lots of club rugby as well as representing my school in this sport. We won both the Borough Championships and Interschools Rugby 7s Cup recently! I am a keen tennis player and as part of my Duke of Edinburgh Award I am volunteering at the tennis club as an assistant coach with younger children. I have a great friendship group and we often get together to watch live rugby locally. I will soon be choosing my GSCE options at school and concentrating on the subjects that I like.

'Will'

When 'Will' was asked what would have made the biggest difference to his time at primary school, he said going to a different school. Initially a very literal response – of course, it would be most different to go to a different school! Having talked through the intention of the question he thought that having clubs would be a good idea. He goes to a couple of Minecraft clubs out of school at the moment.

These are 'Will's' own words:

I am 13 years old and I have autism and ADHD. I like games and computers. I go to secondary school with an SRP (specialist resourced provision) for autism. I love having more advanced maths and science. They have Bunsen burners in the science lab! They have computers too.

These are Eleanor's own words:

I am 13 years old. I live with my dad and older sister, who is in the lower sixth. I've had two cats but the fox got one and the other one had cancer. I am taller than some of my teachers and I love Doc Martins. I have a good memory. My favourite subjects at school are science and history. I also do cooking at school and with one of my friends at their house. My dad is famous for his biscuits and I'm trying to get him to make chocolate chip cookies [rather than oatmeal and raisin]. I go horse riding once a week after school. My favourite colour is pink, or course.

I would change absolutely nothing [about my primary school]. I like primary school and secondary school equally.

My memories of primary school are going swimming, music – this was my favourite, art and *Grendel: A Cautionary Tale about Chocolate*. Do you remember that? That was so much fun. We got to eat chocolate! I remember all my teachers and they all helped me.

So many thanks to the other contributors who also served as the catalyst for this book : Charlie, Maisie, Holly, Tom, Quinn, Logan and Jack.

Reflections

How will you start to gather your pupils' views, thoughts and feelings of school? You may have already started to do so.

Are your pupils' perspectives aligned with the pupils' perspectives in this book?

What are the unique perspectives which your pupils shared?

What is the first thing that you will change in response to your pupils' voice?

Summary

The rise in autism self-advocacy, together with human rights legislation, means that we are becoming increasingly aware of the need to listen to our autistic children and young people. However, many autistic children and young people are not being given the opportunity to share their views, thoughts and feelings of their unique, lived experiences. This means that we may lack an understanding of the support which they need.

The failure to listen to the voices of autistic children and young people continues to impact negatively on their lives and, despite our best endeavours, the experiences and outcomes for autistic children and young people continue to be poor across multiple sectors, including education. To support our pupils, we should make the changes which the pupils themselves request. I stress that adopting an autism-affirming, whole-school approach in response to pupil voice, will benefit autistic and non-autistic pupils alike.

The three houses approach has been effective in uncovering the topics which were important to the pupils. The approach also facilitated the pupils in sharing perspectives on each of the topics. Following analysis of the data, three key themes and a number of sub-themes emerged. Quotes from many pupils from several schools were included to highlight the consistency of the pupils' narrative. This may give us confidence to act and begin to create autism-affirming schools from the pupils' perspectives. I stress throughout this book that it is entirely underpinned by pupil voice.

In this chapter, I have:

Drawn some conclusions on how we may begin to create autism-affirming schools, from our pupils' perspectives.

Highlighted the adaptations and adjustments which were requested by the pupils themselves and may, therefore, give us a unique perspective into what autism-affirming schools should be like.

Shared my personal reflections.

Left the final words to four pupils whose views, thoughts and feelings on their experience of school were the catalyst for this book.

Reference

Milton, D. (2012) On the ontological status of autism: The double empathy problem. *Disability and Society*, 27(6): 883–887.

Appendices

Appendix 1: Individual interview script
Appendix 2: List of books written for and by autistic authors
Appendix 3: All About Me – letter of invitation for families – online only
Appendix 4: All About Me – explanatory presentation for families – online only
Appendix 5: All About Me – an example of the pupil booklet – online only
Appendix 6: All About Me – Pupil characteristics visual prompts Widgit Symbols © Widgit Software Ltd 2002- 2024 www.widgit.com
Appendix 7: All About Me – Strengths visual prompts Widgit Symbols © Widgit Software Ltd 2002- 2024 www.widgit.com
Appendix 8: All About Me – Difficulties visual prompts Widgit Symbols © Widgit Software Ltd 2002- 2024 www.widgit.com

Appendices 3, 4, and 5 are available online only and can be downloaded by following the access instructions at the front of this book.

Appendix 1

Individual interview script

(The interview script is an example of the topics raised in one school. The topics raised in other school contexts may differ. The interview format can be adapted to different topics and contexts.)

Hello, are you feeling ok today?

We met on ... day and we talked about how we could work together to make the school better for you. We thought it would be a good idea to ask you and some of the other children to talk about what they think an autism-affirming school should be like.

Are you ok to talk to me about what you think an autism-affirming school should be like?

Before we start: remember that you don't have to answer all the questions; you can take a break or stop whenever you want; I won't tell the teachers what you say. But I will collect everyone's answers together so we can try and work out what an autism-affirming school should be like as this may help you, your friends and the teachers. I will show your answers to you and you can change your answers if you want to.

Is that ok?

The interview will only begin if the child describes herself/himself as being in the 'green' zone of regulation.

Do you have any questions before we start?

Reveal three houses. Ok, I've got three houses here – the house of good things; the house of worries and the house of dreams. When we talk about anything that you think is going well or is good, we're going to put it in the house of good things. Anything that you are worried about or isn't going well, we're going to put in the house of worries. Anything that you would like us to change to make the school better, we're going to put in the house of dreams.

Do you have any questions about the three houses?

Is there anything that you would like to put in the three houses before we start?

Ok, first of all, let's talk about your friends. Do you have any friends at school? What are their names?

Friends

Is there anything about your friends that is good or going well? We can put this in the house of good things?

Is there anything about your friends that is not going well or that you are worried about? We can put this in the house of worries?

Is there anything that you would like your friends to change? We can put this in the house of dreams.

Now, let's think about break time.

Break

Is there anything about break time that is good or going well? We can put this in the house of good things?

Is there anything about break time that is not going well or that you are worried about? We can put this in the house of worries?

Is there anything that we could change about break time? We can put this in the house of dreams.

Now, let's think about lunch time.

Lunch

Is there anything about lunch time that is good or going well? We can put this in the house of good things?

Is there anything about lunch time that is not going well or that you are worried about? We can put this in the house of worries?

Is there anything that we can change about lunch time? We can put this in the house of dreams.

Homework

What do you think about homework?

Is there anything about homework that is good or going well? We can put this in the house of good things?

Is there anything about homework that is not going well or that you are worried about? We can put this in the house of worries?

Is there anything that we could change about homework? We can put this in the house of dreams.

If you had your own homework rules, would that make homework better?

Teachers

Is there anything about your teachers that is good or going well? We can put this in the house of good things.

Is there anything about your teachers that is not going well or that you are worried about? We can put this in the house of worries.

Is there anything that your teachers could change? We can put this in the house of dreams.

Lessons/learning

What are your favourite lessons?

Are there any lessons that you don't like?

What are these lessons?

Is there anything about your lessons/learning that is good or going well? We can put this in the house of good things.

Is there anything about your lessons/learning that is not going well or that you are worried about? We can put this in the house of worries.

Is there anything that we could change about your lessons/learning? We can put this in the house of dreams.

Are you ok?

We've got more questions to talk about, is that ok?

Now, let's think about the classrooms.

Classroom

Is there anything about the classrooms that is good or going well? We can put this in the house of good things.

Is there anything about the classrooms that is not going well or that you are worried about? We can put this in the house of worries.

Is there anything that we could change about the classrooms? We can put this in the house of dreams.

People who help you at school.

Does anyone help you in school?

Do you have things that help you in the classroom?

Is there anything about this help that is good or going well? We can put this in the house of good things.

Is there anything about this help that is not going well or that you are worried about? We can put this in the house of worries.

Is there anything that we could change about this help? We can put this in the house of dreams.

If your pupil know that they are autistic …

Do you think that the teachers understand about autism?

How do you know this?

Do you think that your friends at school understand about autism?

How do you know this?

Do you think that you understand about autism?

Would you like help to know more about autism?

Finally, is there anything else that you would like to talk about?

Discuss any emergent themes.

Appendix 2

Book list

Blue Bottle Mystery: An Asperger Adventure, Kathy Hoopmann

M in the Middle, The students of Limpsfield Grange and Vicky Martin

M is for Autism, The students of Limpsfield Grange and Vicky Martin

The Secret Life of Rose, Rose Smitten

The Girl with the Curly Hair, Alis Rowe

Can You See Me? Libby Scott and Rebecca Westcott

Frankie's World, Aoife Dooley

Anything But Typical, Nora Raleigh Baskin

All Birds Have Anxiety, Kathy Hoopmann

All Cats Are on the Autism Spectrum, Kathy Hoopmann

Ruby's Worry, Tom Percival

Perfectly Norman, Tom Percival

The Curious Incident of the Dog in the Night-Time, Mark Haddon

It's Raining Cats and Dogs: An Autism Spectrum Guide to the Confusing World of Idioms, Metaphors and Everyday Expressions, Michael Barton

My Awesome Autism, Nikki Saunders

Appendix 6

Visual prompts to support 'Me on the inside'

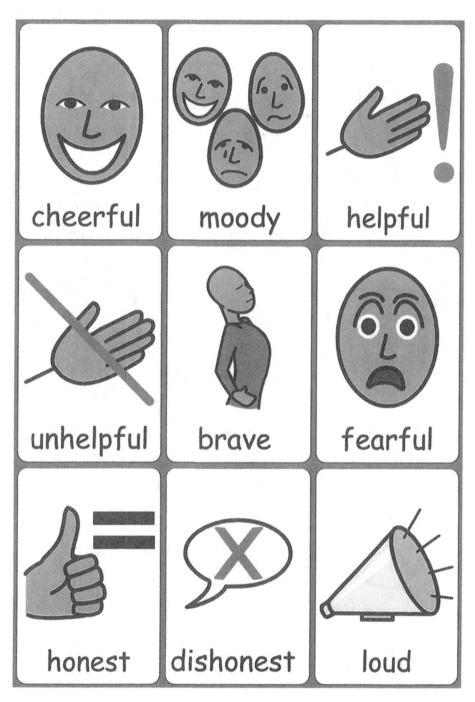

tidy

messy

hardworking

hardworking

active

inactive

sporty

friendly

shy

Copyright material from Melanie Cunningham, Becoming an Autism-Affirming Primary School, 2025, Routledge

confident	gentle	rough
kind	unkind	generous
careful	caring	organised

Copyright material from Melanie Cunningham, Becoming an Autism-Affirming
Primary School, 2025, Routledge

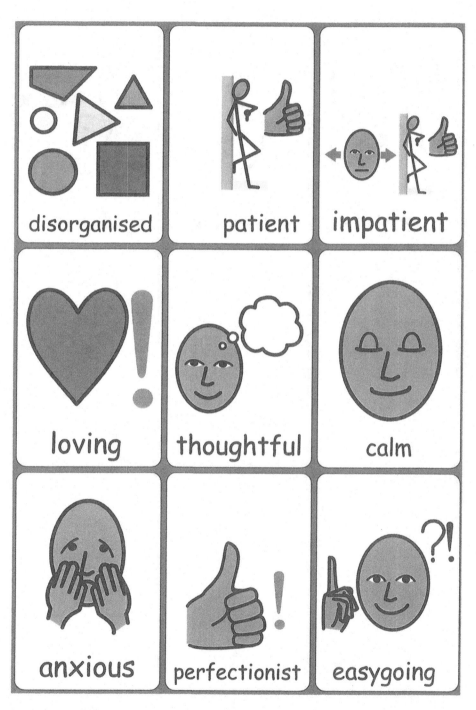

disorganised

patient

impatient

loving

thoughtful

calm

anxious

perfectionist

easygoing

scientific	creative	fair

Appendix 7

Visual prompts to support strengths

dance	technology	crafts
chess	gardening	map reading
handwriting	reading	spelling

counting	puzzles	making animations
designing things	making video movies	spotting train
working out train routes	reading train timetables	working out bus routes

reading   bus

timetables

making

models

using

tablets

collecting

things

electronic

gaming

photography

using gadgets

learning

1 ———
2 ———
3 ———
4 ———
5 ———

facts

helping   with

shopping

laundry

caring for animals

playing musical instruments

Appendix 8
Visual prompts to support difficulties

Copyright material from Melanie Cunningham, Becoming an Autism-Affirming
Primary School, 2025, Routledge

being in crowds

busy

places

understanding personal space

going to the supermarket

Playtime

finding people to play with

playing team games

losing

partner work

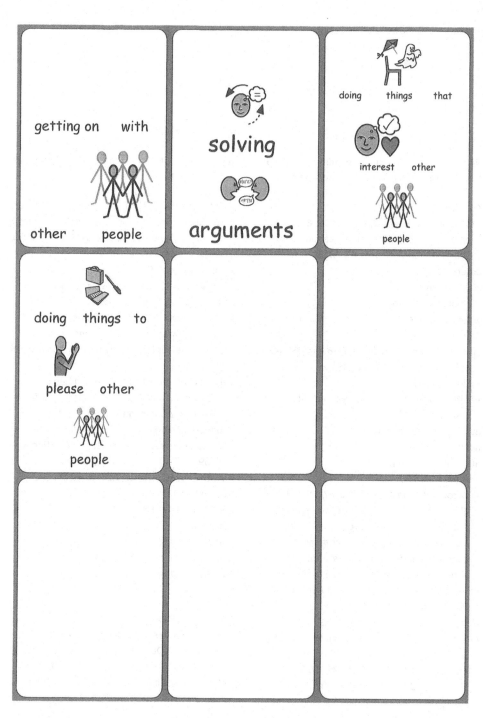

getting on with

other people

solving

arguments

doing things that

interest other

people

doing things to

please other

people

INDEX

Note: For figure citations, page numbers appear in *italics*. For table citations, page numbers appear in **bold**. 'App' is an abbreviation of Appendices.